Dispatches from a
Not-So-Perfect Life

DISPATCHES FROM A NOT-SO-PERFECT LIFE

Or How I Learned to Love
the House, the Man, the Child

FAULKNER FOX

HARMONY BOOKS
NEW YORK

*All the names in this book have been changed except my own.
Everything else is how I remember it.*

⌒◇⌒

Grateful acknowledgment is made to the following for permission to reprint previously published material: **Sarabande Books:** excerpt from the poem "After Detox" from *The Lord and the General Din of the World* by Jane Mead, published by Sarabande Books, Inc. Copyright © 1996 by Jane Mead. Reprinted by permission of Sarabande Books and the author. **Special Rider Music:** excerpt from the song lyric "All Along the Watchtower" by Bob Dylan. Copyright © 1968 by Dwarf Music. All rights reserved. International copyright secured. Reprinted by permission of Special Rider Music.

Published by Harmony Books, New York, New York. Member of the Crown Publishing Group, a division of Random House, Inc.
www.crownpublishing.com
HARMONY BOOKS is a registered trademark and the Harmony Books colophon is a trademark of Random House, Inc.

Printed in the United States of America

Design by Karen Minster

Library of Congress Cataloging-in-Publication Data
Fox, Faulkner.
Dispatches from a not-so-perfect life : or how I learned to love the house, the man, the child / Faulkner Fox.—1st ed.
1. Fox, Faulkner. 2. Wives—United States—Biography. 3. Mothers—United States—Biography. 4. Housewives—United States—Biography. 5. Motherhood. 6. Marriage. I. Title. HQ759 .F69 2003
306.874'3'092—dc21   2003012242

ISBN 1-4000-4939-3

10 9 8 7 6 5 4 3 2 1

FIRST EDITION

✳ FOR GUNTHER ✳

CONTENTS

Dispatches from a Not-So-Perfect Life

INTRODUCTION

When I had a three-year-old and a seven-month-old, I loved my children passionately, and I was also very unhappy. This made me guilty. What did I have to be unhappy about? I had two healthy, beautiful sons; a husband who sometimes got on my nerves but whom I loved; a house that was often dirty but had a lot of potential; an interesting, albeit badly paid teaching job; several hours a week to write; and enough money, at least for the time being. This wasn't the profile of someone who should be weeping inconsolably. It was more like the description of a life many women—myself included some days— would view as near perfect, or at least quite good. So what in the world was wrong?

As I'm prone to do, I turned to books for answers. I read *The Art of Happiness* by His Holiness The Dalai Lama, *Of Woman Born: Motherhood as Experience and Institution* by Adrienne Rich, *Feng Shui: Arranging Your Home to Change Your Life* by Kirsten M. Lagatree, and *Screaming to Be Heard: Hormonal Connections Women Suspect, and Doctors Still Ignore* by Elizabeth Lee Vliet, M.D. I scoured dozens of other spiritual, medical, feminist, nutritional, and self-help titles looking for a solution and a reason for my unhappiness.

I also solicited advice from friends and family. Everyone listened patiently and all had suggestions. No one was objective, of course; I'm not friends with any robots. The people telling me to take Prozac were, basically, on Prozac themselves. My mother persuaded me to get my hormone (she pronounces it "har-mone") levels checked. She often favors biochemical explanations for distress—possibly, in this case, because anything psychodynamic might lead down a road that could implicate her. A priest told me I needed to forgive myself. A man who wanted to sleep with me told me I should have an affair.

But I'm making everyone sound incredibly narrow-minded, some full of raw self-interest. It wasn't like that. I believe my friends and family were genuinely trying to help me, honestly giving me the best advice they had. Who was right? Everyone?

As the books did, most people tended to focus on one arena for change: a psychological shift, a new exercise regimen, antidepressants, weaning, or sending some of the laundry out. Sometimes the same person would focus on an entirely different solution during a second conversation: the benefits of yoga, say, when she had previously talked about the possibility of separating from my kind and well-meaning husband. What package of changes would work for me? I wasn't sure, but here are some of the things I found most interesting and relevant in my reading and conversations:

✳   During their childbearing years, women have, on average, half of the serotonin in their brains that men of the same age do.

✳   There's some kind of new traditionalism afoot, a pressure to have lots of kids and for women to reject the careerism of the 1980s and early 1990s.

✳   Breast-feeding women need to consume 3,300 calories a day.

✳   Sleep deprivation, which is par for the course in early parenting, causes burning eyes, delusions, paranoia, astereognosis (the inability to recognize things by touch), reduced levels of serotonin, and—at least in extremely tired lab rats and dogs—death.*

✳   When two people form a domestic partnership, the one whose outside work is perceived as less important, more flexible, or less likely to make a lot of money is the one who stays home with a sick child. This person also tends to do the lion's share of daily childcare and housework. Nine times out of ten in a heterosexual couple, this person is the woman.

✳   My mother says I've always been a pessimist.

✳   As a group, middle-class and upper-middle-class white women in the Western World have been vaguely dissatisfied to stark raving mad for at least 150 years. Sociodemographically, we're the client base that created psychoanalysis.

---

*   See John Seabrook, "Sleeping with the Baby," *The New Yorker,* November 8, 1999, pp. 56–65.

While I had a lot to think about, I wasn't wondering what was wrong with me full-time, or even very often. I was busy, busier than I'd ever been. I had a baby, a toddler, a teaching job, and a half-done book of poems. Before motherhood if I slipped into a funk (never as deeply as this), I'd go to bed for the day and try to sleep it off. That didn't seem like an option this time. Who could replace me? Even if my husband, sister, and mother working together could, I would have been too guilty to lie in bed when nothing overtly physical was wrong. In retrospect, though, I probably spent many more hours reading, weeping, and talking on the phone than a few days of full-time bed rest would have entailed. I don't know if a brief respite in bed would have cured me, but I bet it would have helped.

I didn't take to bed as a mother because it felt like a betrayal of my responsibilities, whereas worrying and talking felt like coping. And I was breast-feeding so if I wanted to be alone in bed, I'd only be able to do three-hour chunks at a time. Or else cuddle up with my forty-pound breast pump, using it every three hours, then taking the fragile product down to the refrigerator—also not an option that would allow for uninterrupted bed rest.

When I hit my maternal low, I was in a situation that, I think, is considered totally normal for a person who has a baby and a three-and-a-half-year-old: Every day for the past three and a half years, at least one small, cute, and needy person woke me up at 6 A.M. or earlier. More days than not, that person wanted to drink milk from my body. My days struck me as starting under an engine other than my own and pretty much continuing that way all day and all night. Apparently, this was an adjustment I wasn't quite adjusting to. Was this "all" that was wrong?

I decided to do what many middle-class women do nowadays when we're distressed and confused about why: I went to a therapist. Unfortunately, when you most need a therapist, your powers of discrimination may not be at their best. Was Louise Dunlap a good therapeutic match for me? Who knew? I was too desperate to look around.

During our sessions, Louise gave me shopping advice. I'm not a shopper. She asked what I thought about Anne Lamott's new book—I liked it. She asked if I could recommend other books like it for her to read—I could. She told me I needed to make friends with other mothers at the park, but I was afraid of the park and the other mothers who looked as tired and unhappy as I was. Louise encouraged me to "move past" this view.

Surely, this couldn't be worth eighty-five bucks an hour.

In our fourth session, Louise asked to see something I'd written. Two weeks later, she began our session with "So you're not delusional, you can write."

Was this a compliment? It sure didn't hit me in the gut like one. I felt that Louise was trying to suss me out, catch me in a big fat lie. I might have passed this test, but who knew what the next one would be?

"Do lots of your clients lie," I asked, "say they're writers when they're not?"

"Yes," she said. "Fifty percent of the women I see claim to be writers."

Shit, I thought. What I'm doing—in my garage, in sweatpants, often depressed—is so glamorous that half the women in therapy (at least in therapy with Louise) want to, or pretend to, write, too? Whatever happened to the noble dream of being the first woman doctor in the family—helping people, curing sick children?

Maybe those of us in therapy are able to romanticize our unhappiness by thinking it might be connected to the production of art. Depressed yet verbal women, in particular, could be drawn to identify with suicidal writers like Sylvia Plath, Anne Sexton, and Virginia Woolf. *If I have to suffer, goddamnit, I'd better be a genius.* I can definitely see the appeal in these identifications—I've gone through several obsessed-with-Sylvia-Plath phases myself.

Within a few weeks of therapy with Louise, I began to realize what I wanted from her, what would make my time and money seem unwasted, and I asked her for it. I wanted a pie chart of the reasons I was unhappy, something like this: 14% cultural pressure to be a perfect mother; 10% dysfunctional family of origin; 8% biochemical tendency to depression; 14% unequal division of household labor with my husband (I did more); 8% alienation from Texas, where I was currently living; 10% sleep deprivation; 8% hormonal imbalance due to breast-feeding; 6% pessimistic temperament; 10% loss of social power; and 12% no good friends in town.

Louise said I couldn't have this kind of pie chart, that the mind didn't work that way. Why not, damnit? I wanted to know what was wrong with me, in what percentages, so I could fix it. I was willing to concede that certain slices of pie leak into others, but I wanted to know in any given moment who was most relevant to my current despair: Freud, Dr. Spock, or Betty Friedan?

The Dalai Lama says we Americans always want a

cause for our unhappiness, that we are uncomfortable with the mysteries of life. I am American to the bone. I want causes, and then I want solutions.

Louise refused to give me causes or solutions. I can see how this might have been too much to ask, but I don't think it's why our therapy ultimately fizzled out. It fizzled because I began to feel—rather strongly—that Louise thought I was a whiner. About 80 percent of the time, I felt certain Louise was thinking to herself, *Why can't she just get over this and shut up?*

Perhaps Louise was right about certain of my maladaptive obsessions. On the other hand, feminists never "get over" anything. That's where our analytical fervor comes from, as well as our reputation—which I find unfair—for being humorless.

I feel confident in saying that some of what has caused me trouble as a wife and mother comes from our culture. But I also have some "issues" with mothering and wifedom that I suspect are peculiar to me. I don't want to ignore social pressures on women—just the opposite, I want to expose them—but I also don't want to blame the patriarchy for my own idiosyncrasies. I did blame the patriarchy (and my parents) for almost everything throughout my twenties. I'm thirty-nine now, and I'm expecting a more multifaceted lens from myself. When I first started trying to sort out the reasons for my distress as a wife and mother, the most complex model I could visualize was the pie chart.

But a pie chart isn't all that helpful in sorting out a situation like Frank Gilroy's chicken. Frank Gilroy was my husband's boss when our second son was born, and Frank had his own backyard smoker. Three weeks after the birth, he appeared at our back door with a freshly smoked chicken. How kind! How thoughtful! And I was ravenous—I could have torn the chicken leg from wing and devoured it right there on the spot. Frank just smiled as I went on about my hunger and excitement to eat, then delivered the comment that was clearly itching inside him, the sentence designed to let us see the true enormity of his thoughtfulness. "I figured you all might really need this chicken tonight," he said, "since it's Faulkner's teaching day."

Frank was right, in fact, that immediately after Benjamin was born, I taught only on Mondays. It was a low-paid job at the University of Texas that I'd been able to get (with a hand from Frank) because my husband, Duncan, was full-time faculty there. Not that the job felt like anything you'd need insiderism to snag. As an adjunct, I made one-seventh of what Duncan made per course, and he was paid meagerly by most people's professional standards. The great benefit of academia—the one that's supposed to make up for the shitty wages—is flexibility, and Duncan had indeed been able to arrange his schedule so that he could be home with Benjamin on Mondays.

Here was a bone for Frank to chew on: Monday was the *only* day we ever had good food in the house because Duncan had time and the inclination to cook on Mondays. Not that we wouldn't eat up Frank's chicken. We would, and I felt certain it would be tasty. I was extremely grateful to Frank and simultaneously pissed. Where did he get off thinking I was in charge of cooking? Did his assumption have anything to do with how little my postpartum salary was?

If truth be known, I hadn't done much more than boil

water since my oldest son, Joseph, had been born. Since then the cooking had fallen pretty solidly to Duncan. And how in the world could I cook now? I was breast-feeding constantly, taking care of a toddler and a newborn, grocery shopping, cleaning, doing laundry, grading papers, teaching, and preparing a course. I know there are some superwomen out there, but I'm not one of them. With a three-week-old, Monday was the only day I consistently took the time to get dressed. Why bother? I'd have to rip off my shirt about a billion times a day, and it's hot enough in Texas to live in a nursing bra and underwear. I wanted Frank Gilroy to know that Monday was my *best* day, and definitely not the day our family was on the verge of starvation.

Did I explain any of this to him? Of course not. I just took the chicken and let Duncan handle most of the profuse thanking that I, too, could see was necessary. Afterward when I tried to tell Duncan why I was angry, I yearned for a pie chart. But no pie chart is up to the job of explaining accurately what was going on that afternoon—some combination, I'm sure, of self-esteem problems, exhaustion, resentment toward Duncan (he taught two classes that semester and I taught one, yet I was the parent in charge four days of the week while he covered Mondays), and funky breast-feeding hormones on my part; a heavy dose of sexist assumptions by Frank; ingrained gender inequity in the university pay scale; and nothing at all, probably, on the part of the chicken.*

* Women are twice as likely as men to work in low-paid adjunct positions in colleges across the country, while only one-quarter of the highest-paid full professors are women. Suzanne Cleary, "Faculty in Academe," *National Education Association Update*, vol. 4, no. 4 (Sept. 1998).

As a wife and mother, I've experienced dozens of scenarios like this—times when I've felt a mix of emotions, suspected several culprits, and longed for clarity. While I know the perfect pie chart is a strange thing to crave, sometimes I imagine myself as a social scientist in front of a gorgeous visual aid because the stance itself feels so beautifully self-protective. If a particular mothering moment really depresses me—say, a Mommy-and-me sing-along at the library where all the moms look exhausted and bored but also anxious, and some of the kids are antsy, some wild, and none seem to be paying attention to the stern librarian who is playing the Autoharp and singing "Old MacDonald" in a militaristic and off-key way—sometimes I slip into social scientist mode. I watch and take notes, though often just mental ones since my life as the mother of young children has been too hectic at times to have a free hand. The persona of social scientist gives me a purpose, which helps me not to get demoralized, but it also isolates me from other mothers. I've been lonely because of the isolation, yet I've wagered, perhaps wrongly, that isolation in these situations will be less debilitating to me than feeling like "just" a mother.

I think the root of some of the anguish I've perceived in other mothers and within myself on occasions like the sing-along stems from uncertainty about how, exactly, we should be spending our time. *Shouldn't we be doing work the world deems productive and worthy of payment? Certainly, it would be crazy for an American woman to wait for the United States to recognize—and pay women—for mothering. On the other hand, are sing-alongs really necessary? Would our children, who don't seem to be particularly enjoying the Autoharp, be just as well off at daycare without us?*

Except for the seven months immediately after Joseph was born, I've been working or in school while I've had young kids. But I've had flexibility in my work schedule and less childcare than would allow me to work nine-to-five every weekday, so I'm often with Joseph and Ben, now ages five and eight, at some point during regular work hours. As I've moved among the full-time moms and varieties of part-time and flex-time moms like myself, I've been, frankly, terrified by much of what I've seen: unhappy women talking in fake, zombielike, high-pitched voices; whiny, demanding kids; huge bags of diapers and snacks. Rarely is a man present. This is a women's ghetto, albeit a moneyed one.

Initially, I was afraid to ask other mothers how they felt about being in all-women situations with their children. Did they view library sing-alongs as disempowering, or were they simply having fun? Did they feel like less of a person, on occasion, without the job they used to have? Or were they, perhaps, relieved to leave it behind? It seemed presumptuous to ask questions like this to mothers I was just meeting. But I was desperate to know the answers.

I was curious—for personal, political, and social science reasons—how contemporary American mothers felt about ourselves. Take the issue of ambition: How many of us would describe ourselves as ambitious? Had our ambitions changed since having children? To help me answer these and other burning questions I had, I eventually began to interview a wide range of mothers, but I knew I was no sociologist. This is primarily a book from my perspective. Still, I am someone who makes sense of the world by talking to other women. The days when I was too fearful to broach true feelings about motherhood and domestic life with the women around me were some of the most isolating of my life. I began conducting interviews out of loneliness, curiosity, and sympathy and also because I wanted to see how much of what I was feeling was "just me" and how much was shared by others.

While these certainly haven't been my only emotions, I've felt split, ambivalent, and guilty as a mother, to a degree I never felt beforehand. If these feelings are simply part of being human, then mothering has made me more human. To the extent that they are difficult, sometimes excruciating, emotions to sit with, mothering has made me wonder, *What's wrong with me?* more often than I used to.

I don't hover endlessly in self-doubt, though, especially if I'm getting enough sleep. *What's wrong with this, them, him, or her?* is likely to follow close on the heels of any initial look inward. Sometimes I flip back and forth really fast—it's me, it's them; it's me, it's my husband; it's my mother, it's me; it's those exhausted but competitive women at the park, it's me; it's me, it's our pernicious, sexist culture.

It's important to me not to blame the wrong people or structures for the wrong things, which is why the pie-chart concept appealed to me in the first place. Overall, I've been somewhat surprised by which domestic situations have unnerved me most. They haven't always been the ones I would have predicted, pre-motherhood. Diapering, for example, turned out to be a complete non-problem. Amazingly enough, I really don't mind having poop on my hands. In fact, the actual work of mother-ing—the tasks I do with my young children like feeding and bathing them, reading to them, brushing their teeth—rarely fill me with the kind of dismay I felt regard-ing Frank Gilroy's chicken. I love my children dearly, and I don't love Frank Gilroy, but that doesn't explain every-thing.

My sons have unquestionably stoked the sleep-deprivation fire, a force that makes literally everything in a day harder to handle, but especially now that they're older, my major domestic problem areas seem fairly detached from my own children. Once after I'd returned from a horrendous birthday party featuring a filthy blow-up pool with at least thirty toddlers slipping, falling, and crying in the water while their parents stood around, long-faced in the broiling sun, trying to connect with one another without acknowledging how truly awful the event was, Duncan said, "Parenting is an antidote to par-enting." What he meant is that the actual love and work of being alone with your children can heal you from the hell of various public parenting situations. He was right, I thought, and what I wanted as detox from the party was to get everyone into pajamas and lie around calmly, read-ing or chatting. Possibly, I would have been more quickly restored if I'd read alone for an hour or so, but being with my children, per se, was not what had me so strung out right then.

In this book, I describe the particular trouble spots that have been hardest for me as a wife and mother—maintaining a sense of myself as an individual; work ambitions vs. desire to be a focused *über*-mom; negotiat-ing pregnancy advice literature and birth options without resorting to crippling self-blame; barbed negotiations over housework and childcare with my husband; judgmentalism at baby-and-me classes and preschool potlucks; and realizing I didn't have to radically alter my personality for my children's sake. Rather than making a pie chart of the reasons for my domestic difficulties, I tell stories and raise questions, keeping one eye on myself—is this just me?—and one eye on elements of the larger social world: What's Frank Gilroy's investment in my being the family cook? At every turn, I explore which aspects of the house-man-child package feel most oppressive and which most redemptive.

Certainly, there is no global mothering experience, and I would be loath to claim that I'm living it. On the other hand, the sum of what happens to any one of us is never just personal. This book is my story, and it's idiosyncratic, but I've been compelled to write it out of a sense that the isolation, conflict, and love I've felt as a wife and mother are anything but limited to me. I've wanted to tell the truth—in writing—in the hope that my story could help other women feel less alone, less crazy, and possibly less guilty.

ONE

House, Man, Child

I began to fantasize about being in a house with a man and a child when I was twenty-three. It was an ambivalent fantasy, in terms of motherhood; I wasn't sure if I was the child's mother. I was the man's lover, that much was clear, and the child looked like him. Maybe I was the live-in mother, or maybe I was a frequent guest and sex partner who went home to her own bachelorette pad in the city.

The fantasy opens with me in the foreground, working at a computer beside a large glass window. It's dusk and a purplish blue tinges the sky. I can see the ocean just outside the window and over a cliff—wild, angry, gorgeous. To my right at an open kitchen area, an attractive blond man is deveining shrimp for the paella he's preparing while listening to Miles Davis. The music is low (out of respect for me), and as the man has anticipated, it doesn't bother me. I like the sad and lovely trumpet drifting my way. At once, I feel relaxed and incredibly focused on work I love doing.

Between the man and me on a clean and bare floor, a blond four-year-old plays with wooden trucks. He loads tiny logs into the truck beds, then takes them out and splays them on the floor like a fan. He's happy without ever being loud, and he doesn't get up. He simply sits and plays.

Meanwhile, I keep working. There's no reason for me to stop. My work is going well, and paella takes a long time to cook. Eventually, when the sky is dark, I do stop, and we—meaning the man and I—eat at a table beside huge windows that face the sea. We drink red wine, and there are candles on the table, the kind that bob in oil inside clear glass cylinders.

I never see the child when I imagine our meal. Maybe he continues to play quietly into the night, or maybe he has already put himself to bed. I never see it in my vision, but surely the man must have placed a bowl of apples, a peanut butter and jelly sandwich, a piece of shrimp from the paella beside the child at some point. I might even have given him a mug of milk. Pouring luscious whole milk into a cool blue mug, bending down once to place it on the floor—I could do that. I could do it and still be myself.

✳✳✳

In my real life at twenty-three, I lived alone, with chin-length brown hair, in a New Orleans apartment recently inhabited by two heroin addicts. A dozen needles lay in the weeds beside a banana tree in the backyard. My downstairs neighbor was a woman who seemed to be suffering from posttraumatic stress syndrome caused by WWII. Often I would wake around 4 A.M. to her yelling or loud moaning. Sometimes Irene spoke in German; other times she would scream, in clear, crisp English:

"Goddamn Jesus! Goddamn Jesus!" Irene didn't have a car, and I drove her to Steak and Egg on occasion, the only place I ever knew her to go. We sat in the grimy, maroon plastic booths drinking iced tea and smoking cigarettes. Irene was very lonely. So was I.

It was 1987, and I'd moved to New Orleans to study voodoo and witchcraft. I did this by interviewing and apprenticing myself to a variety of practitioners. I wasn't sure how much of my interest was academic and how much was personal. When I told one rootworker that I was doing research for a book I might write on women and magic, she said, "God sent you here, and you've come for a love potion." She was right, I remember thinking.

I felt myself to be living provisionally in New Orleans. Interviewing people, typically older ones whose lives I viewed as "real," contributed to this sense. I was an apprentice, an interviewer, someone who watched others to see how life could be done rather than someone who actually lived herself. I had a student's view of the world: Nothing counted yet, I was just gathering information.

"It never occurred to me that I was living a real life there," Joan Didion wrote of herself in New York City at twenty. "It was difficult in the extreme for me to understand those young women for whom New York was not simply an ephemeral Estoril but a real place, girls who bought toasters and installed new cabinets in their apartments."* I felt similarly in New Orleans. I never would have bought a toaster. I had no small appliances, and

---

* Joan Didion, "Goodbye to All That," *Slouching Towards Bethlehem* (New York: Farrar, Straus and Giroux, 1967).

almost no furniture—a mattress, a card table, two attached seats from an out-of-business movie theater. New Orleans seemed the obvious place for me to live since I wanted to write and study voodoo, but I didn't know how long I'd stay, how long the romance of New Orleans would last. When I left, I didn't want to be weighed down.

At the same time, I was curious about the girls with toasters. Were they happier than I was? It was unnerving to have such a tenuous, if romantic, attachment to my life. True, I met someone fascinating at least once a week and because I wore my interviewer's cloak, I got to skip the chitchat and move right to the questions that interested me most: What happens when we die? Is revenge ever okay? When people say "It was like magic," what was it really, and how did it work? These people weren't friends, though; I typically saw them just once. Intimacy was largely missing in my life, as was stability. Would I always sleep on the floor, support myself through a variety of low-paying and ever-shifting jobs, and fraternize primarily with a disturbed neighbor? I hoped not.

I knew I wasn't ready yet, but eventually, motherhood might provide me with a richer, more grounded connection to the world. How could it not? It would bring me to the hub of life; I would create life. How extraordinary, how transformative! And yet when I thought about the mothers I'd had the opportunity to observe in action, they didn't strike me as more rooted or wise about creation than anyone else. If anything, those with young children seemed less so. They had to wipe up too much.

I started taking long walks every afternoon through the tony uptown neighborhood adjacent to my own.

Sometimes I hardly noticed my surroundings, so fully inhabiting my seaside fantasy of man and child that everything else went blank. But then I'd pass a particularly charming house, one elaborately decorated for whatever holiday was in the air—paper skeletons dancing from the porch rafters, glittery turkeys pasted on the windows with "Lulu" and "Charles" scrawled at the bottom—and I'd be wrested back to New Orleans, or rather, my imaginings of it. *What was the mother of the charming house doing now? How did she feel? Did a man ever cook paella for her while she worked?* I doubted it.

If you weren't in fantasy land, it seemed that some rather heavy trade-offs might be involved to live in a house with a man and a child. While I began to think I might eventually want the full life I envisioned inside a carefully festooned house, I didn't want to be the one to create it. All the trips to the drugstore to buy glue sticks and tissue paper, which struck me as likely to be exhausting, would be the least of it. I wanted to have plenty of time alone, and I didn't want to be lonely. Who could I be and accomplish this? A spinster aunt who lived in the attic and came down occasionally to help with homework and sing old camp songs? A single woman who visited a man and a child by the sea, then got the hell out before morning?

In truth, I knew nothing about the women in the houses I passed. I couldn't even see them. Uptown New Orleans is an oddly enclosed world. No one was ever on the porch, and the heavy green shutters were always closed. Perhaps people got used to shutting out the oppressive heat, or possibly some fear of crime kept them locked inside. I didn't know anything about these people; I could only imagine, based on what I saw on the porch—

kid bikes, abandoned tea parties for dolls, expensive jogging strollers.

When my boss at the tutoring agency where I worked, Caroline DuChamp, invited me to her shotgun house on Prytania Street, I was thrilled. Caroline was thirty, and she had a two-year-old daughter. Finally, I'd get an inside look at young motherhood.

While Caroline was home with her child quite a bit, she was no full-fledged stay-at-homer. She ran a successful business, charging $25 an hour for my tutoring services, and paying me $11. If I had baby-sat her daughter, she wouldn't have paid me anything near the $14 an hour she paid herself for every hour I worked. Perhaps I should view Caroline as a role model, a mother who had a flexible and lucrative career. But I didn't want to run a tutoring agency. On the other hand, the three part-time jobs I currently had—teaching French at a Catholic boys' school, conducting weekend tours at the Voodoo Museum, and tutoring for Caroline—netted me less than $8,000 per year. Did Caroline know something I didn't?

If I did have a child, I could hardly drag her to the cemetery where I took Parisian tourists each Saturday to pay tribute at Marie Laveau's grave. My own spiritual beliefs were in flux, but I wouldn't want to take the chance that an unsettled ghost, hovering around the tombs, could curse my baby. If my child fell ill in a more traditional manner, I had no health insurance. Clearly, my life would have to change if I became a mother. I was eager to check in on Caroline's life and see if I could gather any tips for possible future use.

The occasion at Caroline's was a thank-you luncheon for the tutors, all single young women like me. Caroline served chicken salad, globbed with mayonnaise, and lukewarm potato soup. Cold or hot, I remember thinking of the soup—either way would be fine—but the in-between was so unsettling. Had she not had time to chill the soup because of her daughter? Her daughter was nowhere to be seen. The luncheon was a "special event," Caroline announced; we were special enough to warrant a baby-sitter's expense. But her child's existence seemed to dominate the house anyway. Toys were pushed into corners, but there were so many. A Disney sing-along machine fell off one precarious stack during lunch and began to squeak, in fake mouse tones, "Three blind mice, three blind mice . . ." We all laughed warmly, but I was thinking, *I'd go mad in a house like this.*

Caroline had invited a few of her friends, mothers with young children, to join us tutors. They seemed over-joyed to be at a grown-up luncheon. An intense-looking woman from New Jersey said she'd never left her sixteen-month-old before. "I feel giddy! I can't believe I'm here. And I'm drinking wine—think of that!" She closed her eyes and took a long, luxurious sip.

An hour later, after considerably more wine, she seemed less content. "I'm going to New Jersey next week," she told the table. "Joe says we can't afford it. Well, I *need* to see my family. I didn't ask to come here, to leave my job and my life. I'm going all right, on a Grey-hound bus. It'll take forty-two hours. Can you imagine? Me on the bus with the baby? Joe thinks I'm crazy, but he won't pay for the airplane ticket."

I was horrified by her account. Did she love this man? How could he hold money over her like this? In 1987! It was late by the time she finished her story, nearly three, and still the mothers made no gesture toward leaving. How long could they stay away from their lives, lingering in the specialness of adult women's conversation, however depressing the content?

I didn't hang around to find out. I thanked Caroline for lunch and practically ran out her door, away from the drunk mothers, the plastic toys, the bad soup. I was pissed at Caroline for making money off my labor—a fact that chicken salad could hardly amend—but I sure didn't want to change places with her or her friends. My shitty little apartment had never seemed so welcoming. I lay on my mattress on the floor and counted my blessings.

Meanwhile, I kept having my paella-by-the-sea fantasy. My child, if I had one, wouldn't play with unsightly plastic things, and my man, when I found him, wouldn't put me on a bus. I'd drive my own damn car, or fly my own damn plane. Where were the good men, the ones who respected a woman's autonomy? A friend of my sister's told her they were in Shelburne Falls, Massachusetts.

I flew up to visit my sister, who lived in nearby Northampton, and we drove to Shelburne Falls one winter afternoon. Oddly, we saw no males at all except one man burning leaves in his yard and another sliding pizzas into an oven in an Italian restaurant. They were both well over fifty. Too old, we thought. So it was back to our daydreams for both of us, and single life in the tiny, ill-furnished New Orleans apartment for me. For my sister, Celia, three years my junior, bachelorette life took place in a ramshackle one-room cabin between a junkyard and the Connecticut River.

Celia lived in that cabin for eight years, and I visited

her often. In 1991, we celebrated Anita Hill Day there instead of Christmas with our friend Melinda. The three of us decorated Celia's ficus tree with pictures of Anita that we'd clipped from *Newsweek* and *Time,* then burned the images we'd collected of Clarence Thomas in the woodstove. We gave one another *Thelma and Louise* T-shirts. We were all looking for a good man, and at the same time we felt compelled to celebrate women who stood up against bad men, however high the cost.

Anita Hill Day at Celia's cabin was home, as deeply as I'd ever felt it, yet I was sad and lonely that Christmas, not to mention angry. Were the only cultural options—for holidays, as well as life in general—feminist boycott or acquiescence to some package of horrors? It appeared so when I was twenty-six.

The beauty of my paella fantasy, as I saw it in my mid-twenties, was that it held out an alternative vision of life with a man and a child, one I'd never seen in practice. Until I could figure out how to attain it, I'd go on with my single life, critiquing whatever I saw as oppressive. The critiquing was part of how I figured I'd get what I wanted. If you can't pinpoint what's wrong—with typical male-female relationships, in this case—how can you construct something different? But the relentless critiquing was exhausting and often demoralizing. By contrast, my fantasy gave me hope; it was the lighthouse I saw in the distance when reality, through my twenty-something lens, looked like women getting screwed at every turn.

At twenty-three, even at twenty-six, I'd never seen a woman do her own work (excluding housework, of course) at home while men were there. When my father came home from work as an executive at our town's paper mill each day, my mother immediately stopped making organizational phone calls for the Parent-Child Development Center she had founded and aimed a series of solicitous questions his way: "How was your day?" "Can I get you a Scotch and soda?" "Are you hungry— dinner will be ready soon."

All the women I saw during my childhood and adolescence stopped work or leisure when a man came home. *Quick, focus on him!* seemed to be the mantra playing in their heads. Men, apparently, didn't hear a reciprocal chant. The kinder ones would get up and help at the sight of a woman saddled with heavy groceries, but if there were no evident packages, a man's eyes could stay glued on the committee report or the ball game. This struck me as unfair, and I wanted what the men had.

My fantasy self had it. She worked in the same room with a man and a child (the dream house, as I saw it clearly, only had one room), and she was neither guilty nor distracted. Plus it was dinnertime. Whose work or leisure is important? The person who gets to keep doing it while someone else cooks dinner. Forget a multiroom mansion; my fantasy centered on something I suspected was even harder to achieve: a sense of entitlement in the presence of a man and a child.

✳✳✳

In my real life with children and a man, I've needed—and been fortunate enough to have—more than one room. At thirty-nine, I live with my family in a multiroom bungalow, and I work in a garage out back when I'm not teaching. Our house faces a busy street in Austin, Texas, instead of fronting the ocean, but stylistically, it could be a beach cottage. For most of our seven years at this address, I've shared the garage with Patrick, an Irish waiter who rented an efficiency on one side of the building while I worked in the smaller adjacent office. Patrick's side had the bathroom, so if I needed to pee while working in my office, I went in a red bucket covered by a plastic toilet seat my mother got from a boat supply company, then dumped it out the window.

"You're so country!" my friend Monise, who was also raised in small-town Virginia, exclaimed when I told her about my bucket. I viewed my actions as more desperate, though, than country. If I went into the house (where we have a working toilet), I might run into my youngest son and his baby-sitter, upsetting him or myself, and certainly getting caught up in the domestic scene I was trying to cordon off for a few hours while I practiced my chosen profession in the garage. Peeing in a bucket seemed preferable.

When Patrick moved back to Ireland, I started to fantasize about taking over the whole garage. Patrick had loved the Pogues. He'd ramp up his stereo full blast and sing along, so I took to wearing earplugs while I worked. It had seemed a small price to pay, since Patrick was funny and kind, and he always paid his rent. Plus I like the Pogues—their fuck-you righteousness makes me feel young. What music would a new tenant play? I began to wonder. What use might he or she make of overheard intimacies gleaned from my garage phone calls to friends? Perhaps most important, how long before I was caught red-handed with my bucket?

Patrick's apartment needed repainting, and this bought me some time to think. I picked a pale blue color called

"Port of Call," then moved a futon over and hung a poster of sailboats off the coast of North Carolina on the wall. I used the bathroom.

"What are you doing?" Duncan asked when he caught me moving a box of dusty cassettes out to Patrick's former apartment. He walked out with me and noted that the garage was starting to look strangely like the apartment I'd lived in when he met me: books and papers strewn everywhere on the left, a bare mattress on the right. Come to think of it, the garage—as I was fixing it—looked somewhat like all the places I'd lived before marriage and motherhood: the upper-rear apartment in New Orleans, my fourth-floor place in Richmond, and the tree-house-like room above my landlord's garage in New Haven where I'd lived when I met Duncan. They were all adjunctive spaces, rooms tucked behind and above other people's more established lives. "Are you trying to go back in time?" Duncan asked.

It was a good question. I felt penned in by my current life, and I didn't know why. The house was always a mess; its panoply of toys (plastic, wooden, cloth, and neon), dirty socks, photos to be sorted, junk mail, mangled sippy cups with no lids, half dried-up Play-Doh in Ziploc bags, two sad Beta fish swimming in plastic jars with scummy water and fake coral, and dozens of pecans saved in a bag for cooking that would never happen overwhelmed and depressed me. I'd tried different strategies—give lots away, clean up each night, let it all go and work your ass off on Saturday, label drawers with taped-on pictures so the kids will know where things go—and the house still won. On an average day, our place made Caroline's in New Orleans, as I recalled it, seem like a serene, Buddhist temple. My garage office, while brimming with slightly different objects, was no neater. Amidst the chaos in office and home, fiendishly long to-do lists got moved from surface to surface. What were all these tasks pressing on my mind? I just wanted to lie on the mattress in the cool blue room and look at the boats.

"If we lived on the ocean, I wouldn't have to do this," I told Duncan, and then I felt like a dog. We live in Austin because Duncan is a professor here. He knows I don't like Austin—it's inland and dusty, plus far from both my tidewater family and our northeastern friends—and we're trying to move. At the moment, though, I felt guilty about not renting the apartment, and I was trying to slough off some blame on Duncan. "I'm sorry," I said, "I just love this room, and I don't want to give it up yet."

"Okay," he returned, "but it's not 1990. I'll be upset if you have sex out here with a bass player or a tortured poet."

I said I planned to work, use the bathroom, and maybe do some yoga, but then I felt compelled to mention the backyard lore concerning our neighbor across the alley. When Kim developed Chronic Fatigue Syndrome, she banished her husband, Chuck, to a quickly converted toolshed out back. She couldn't sleep, apparently, with Chuck in the house. Within a month, Beverly, who lived in the apartment directly on Chuck and Kim's right, was sneaking away from her own snoring husband to join Chuck in the yard.

The yard is dangerous, not quite domesticated. "I might want to sleep out here some nights," I said, "if I'm working well."

"I'm afraid you won't come back," Duncan replied.

"I'll be close by," I joked, but he didn't laugh.

✳✳✳

From the kitchen, I can see the garage clearly, and sometimes I miss it. Doing dishes or setting the table, I'll look across the yard with the treehouse Duncan built, the herb and flower garden where we buried our sons' placentas—Joseph's under rosemary, Benjamin's under rose—to the bright blue door of the garage. If I were in there now, I'll think, I could sit quietly instead of bustling. An image might take hold of me, carry me somewhere magical, somewhere coastal.

From the garage, I often miss the house and the life it holds. My sons visit frequently on the days when I'm working in the afternoons, seeking permission or simply escaping from Daddy or the baby-sitter. They run at full-tilt the twenty-five yards separating house and garage, bare feet padding on the dirty brick path. In Patrick's ex-apartment, they jump on the futon and dance wildly to an old Rick James cassette I have, then race over to the office side and uncap all my pens and smell them, exclaiming over the especially yucky ones. They lounge on the floor and eat rice cakes, leaving pieces all around, then beg me to search for Pokémon figures on the Internet. I love these visits. Except when I don't love them.

In the garage my sons especially like to make drawings, which I hang on the wall. We form the Scotch tape curls together, my bigger fingers guiding their smaller ones. When my oldest son, Joseph, was five, he did a portrait of me shooting a bow and arrow. He gave me huge orange eyes and amazingly long arms. "Mommy dressed like Robin Hood," he directed me to write underneath. Benjamin, at almost three, was just moving beyond "scribble-scrabble," as Joseph calls it. The day Joseph envisioned me as Robin Hood, Benjamin drew a robot with vampire teeth: a purple box with dots for eyes and a nose, then two upside-down triangles in the mouth position. "This guy keeps bad guys away," he said proudly. Talk about useful art; I posted it immediately above my door.

I didn't want my sons to leave that afternoon; I hugged them and smelled their hair. I signaled to Duncan, who was watering his oregano, that it was okay, they could stay a few more minutes. Still, I felt torn. I don't work in the garage that many hours per day—four or five, tops. Our children are not in full-time childcare, and I teach poetry at the university. There are always meetings and errands, a car inspection, a dentist's appointment, a child's birthday party gift to buy. *I sound so middle-class and suburban; what do I have to complain about? My life is good, and yet I'm often rushing and irritated.* That day, the irritation landed squarely on Duncan. It was his afternoon; he was in charge. If he left the boys with me to go running (he already had his running clothes on), I'd be resentful even if I loved every minute of their company. Work is work, a deal struck with a partner is a deal, and family time is family time. The distinctions seem all-important to me. That's why I live in the house and work in the garage.

"Stop watering," I shouted, and Duncan did. He took the boys to the park, and I missed all three of them, watching their backs move away from me.

✳✳✳

Sometimes I get lonely in the house, even when it's full of people I love dearly. What am I lonely for? Is it Duncan as lover, the raw smell of his chest when we were the only ones? It's so easy to forget his body when I'm surrounded by the bodies of my children—active, sweet smelling, miraculously unlined. They jostle and wiggle on the floor, they wear boots on their hands, they jump on my back and demand that I shout "Neigh, neigh!" At moments like these, my children are sheer, irrepressible joy, and I smile as widely as I ever have. My husband is subtler and more complex, easier to overlook. I can miss him, acutely, when he's standing right there.

Perhaps I miss my son Joseph, when he was the only one—my first baby, my world—for almost three years. I was completely engaged with him, night and day. I'm not sure this was healthy; certainly it was compelling, rich, and exhausting. I know I miss sweet Benjamin even when he's sleeping just upstairs. He's the child who has never been an only, the one I've always split my attention toward. If I could just go back to his babyhood and take it more slowly, with less guilt about Joseph's jealousy and more attention to the moment. I miss the deep attentiveness I had one fall afternoon five years ago when Benjamin slept in my arms as I graded papers on the trash can beside me, the only surface I could reach without waking him. I was doing two things, but it was only two, and my mind was unusually calm, full of love and appreciation for my child. How can this peace be so rare?

Possibly, I miss myself—a grounded and receptive incarnation, rather than the pinched, sleep-deprived, rushing person I know myself to be more often than not. All I can say for sure is, I'm lonely. But I effectively have four-fifths of my paella fantasy in the flesh now: house, man, children, a self who works with focus. The only element obviously missing is the ocean view. Not that I advocate measuring life against fantasy (a move that always seems to lead to unhappiness, yet many of us keep doing it anyway), but if I did measure my life at thirty-nine against my girlish daydream, I couldn't help but recognize that I was doing pretty well. I had been young when I concocted my fantasy, but its goal—an end to loneliness without a huge cost to the self—still struck me as desirable. So what was wrong?

Of course I knew, even at twenty-three, that my fantasy was hopelessly nuclear despite the uncertainty about my dream self's biological motherhood. The traditionalism of my fantasy embarrassed me then, and it embarrasses me now. House, man, child—we're all trained to want this package from the day that very first infant dress is wrangled over our squirming female bodies. No wonder I was lonely. The nuclear package wasn't enough.

I knew myself to miss Renata, my friend in New York, with an intensity that could take my breath away. She and I could circle some knotty truth for hours—nudging, speculating, moving quickly between past and present, others and ourselves, abstraction and detail—until we came to a deeper understanding that made us feel joyful, glad to be human. I have several friends like Renata, dispersed all over the country. I have my sister and my brother. We visit and we talk on the phone, but I long for more.

I also missed the greater political and community engagement I'd had before motherhood, the hours I'd spent with other people working to make the world better, as we perceived it. Who told me to stop? No one, of course; it felt like a simple question of time, of not having enough. And I hadn't stopped entirely. I still took my children to the occasional anti–death penalty rally, wrote editorials against capital punishment, encouraged my students to question authority, gave money to lefty organizations, and donated items from our overstuffed house to the local battered women's shelter. But these efforts paled in comparison to the political activities I'd thrown myself into before motherhood. In Austin, the city I'd moved to while pregnant and inhabited for eight years, I still felt strangely unconnected. Instead, I felt like a woman in a house with a man and children, and alternately, a woman in a garage by herself.

When I decided to say "I'm lonely" out loud to Duncan one night two years ago as we cleaned the kitchen, me wiping the counters while he scrubbed pots, he answered defensively. Duncan has come to know me as the person who blames him for living in Austin, away from old friends and family other than our own nuclear selves. "We need to make an effort," he said, "have people over."

This was not what I had in mind. I felt that my loneliness came from some complex bundle, a personal or structural sickness perhaps: the disturbing inability to feel connected to loved ones who were standing right by me because endless domestic tasks—laundry, dishes, trash, vaccinations, taxes, cleaning the fish bowls—seemed to be always calling my name; a dearth of wandery, deep conversations with those who knew me well; and inadequate involvement in the social movements I cared about. An evening of chitchat with relative strangers wouldn't alleviate any of this. In truth, the majority of social events I'd attended since Joseph's birth made me feel lonelier. Part of this was due to the fact that the people in our circle of neighborhood friends socialized entirely as a family unit. My theory as to why people insisted on an unrelenting all-of-us-in-the-minivan approach to social life was that (a) they felt so guilty about working that they were driven to take their children everywhere they went when not working; or (b) if one parent—the mother, in every case I could think of—had cut her work back severely in order to spend more time with the children, then the family couldn't afford the disposable income to pay a baby-sitter. Whatever the reason, I found the setup frustrating and demoralizing.

"Do you realize we've never once been invited to an adults-only cocktail party," I'd pointed out to Duncan, "the kind my parents had all the time in the sixties?"

"You can't mean you want to bring back those dysfunctional events," he'd replied.

Point taken. But it still bugged me that no one we knew with children invited me anywhere *as a person*. They invited me, I thought, because I was the nondivorced, heterosexual mother of children the same age as their own. What kind of a basis for friendship was this? At the various brunches, picnics, and kid birthday parties we attended at least once a week and hosted about once a month, I found it impossible to talk to any adult for more than one minute and simultaneously upsetting that I couldn't focus on my own children without feeling rude toward the other adults. Even more hideous, other people's children frequently seemed to break something or hit one of mine. Why participate? I'd so much rather play quietly with Joseph and Benjamin, then watch *ER* with Duncan.

But I felt guilty about my asocial tendencies, afraid they were depriving my children. "Don't they see kids all day?" I'd tried to argue to Duncan. "Why do we have to invite more over after hours?"

"It's not the same," he'd say, and I knew it wasn't. So on the night when I proclaimed my loneliness, I thought—after an initial surge of reluctance—why not view the situation simply? I was lonely, and my kids needed socialization. A dinner party seemed utterly reasonable.

As soon as I told Duncan I was on board, I started to dread the effort. What would we cook? How much time would it take to minimally straighten the chaos? Our time seems so precious; this is unquestionably part of what ails me. Why do something on purpose that would cause more domestic work, a time-sucking arena both of us claim to despise?

As a low-energy compromise, we settled on a potluck. Others would bring salad, bread, and dessert, and we would make the main dish. It definitely wouldn't be paella.

✳✳✳

Two nights later at 5 P.M., I was putting a wrinkled red tablecloth on the dining room table, a hand-me-down piece of furniture we never use except to pile up mail. I'd temporarily shoved the mail into a brown paper bag and stuffed it in the closet. Duncan was doing food prep in the kitchen, and the kids were parked on the sofa watching PBS.

"Mommy, *Arthur*'s over. Can we watch *Wishbone,* too?" Benjamin asked.

"Yes," I said, "today you can."

"Hooray!" they both shouted. Mommy was busy. It was a PBS bonanza.

"Did you get any lemons?" Duncan called from the kitchen.

"Shit, I forgot. Can you do without?"

"The chicken will be a lot better with lemon."

"Make it less good. There's no time now."

Why were we rushing so much? Who were we trying to impress? Our guests were all parents. They were all busy. But their houses seemed cleaner than ours. What, exactly, were we doing wrong?

"What do I do with these?" Duncan asked, holding up four plastic bowling pins and a witch's hat.

"Throw them in the closet," I said. "Shut the door quick before everything falls out."

"This is so much work," Duncan groaned, and I noted how exhausted he looked. We're tired all the time now. "Why are we even doing this?" he continued. "I just want to relax, maybe watch a video."

"We don't have any friends. That's why we're doing it."

"I don't even know if I like these people. Let's just get it over with so we can go to bed."

I thought of ruffling Duncan's hair or kissing his cheek in sympathy, but turned to the dishes instead. "You keep doing the food, and I'll clean," I barked. "I'm quicker and a lot less thorough."

Duncan went back to the garlic he was mincing. Thawing chicken breasts floated in a bowl beside him. "You should've seen Connor's house last week. It was trashed," he said.

"Really?" I asked, excitedly. "How so?" Connor and his wife, Sarah, were two of the guests we were expecting.

"Clothes everywhere, papers on the floor, lots of dirty dishes. A total mess."

"Sounds like our house."

"Yeah, but they have cats."

"Oh," I said, "cats. That must have been really bad."

When Connor, Sarah, and their girls arrived at five-thirty, our house looked less cluttered than usual, though I certainly wouldn't have called it clean. Still, it was clear that we'd made an effort. I'd put flowers on the table and Al Green on the stereo. He crooned, "I'm so tired of being alone, I'm so tired of on-my-own . . ."

Mostly, we listen to Raffi at our house with an occasional blast of Bob Marley. But these potlucks are where we adults like to show our musical proclivities, a bit of our pasts since none of us is up on current music. If we were at Connor and Sarah's, the music would definitely be mid-'80s Argentinean. Connor lived in Argentina for seven years. At Rick and Thea's—they arrived with their two sons a few minutes after Sarah and Connor—the music would probably be Dire Straits or Sting.

We're all sort of stuck in the '80s. "I lost track in 1989," Duncan likes to say about music, clothes, and popular culture in general. For the festive but casual occasion that constitutes a potluck, some of us, I realized, had dressed like weathered versions of who we might have been in the 1980s. Thea, who'd lived in Santa Fe, wore a tie-dye dress; Connor sported beads from Chile; Duncan, in a wrinkled button-down and jeans, could pass for a graduate student despite the few more wrinkles around his eyes; Rick was decked out in Patagonia (maybe he'd actually made it as far as the '90s); and I wore a faded black T-shirt and differently faded black pants, evocative, perhaps, of a more urban and cynical past.

While Duncan and I cooked, the kids ran around in the backyard, and the adults clustered in the kitchen chatting about our children's preschools, the shopping mall that was supposed to be built a few blocks away, and the Baptist church that had recently had its expansionist desires defeated by the city council. We all drank Amstel Light, and Connor had brought a bottle of tequila. Everyone except Thea had a shot, but there was no chance that anyone would get loaded. This was a family dinner, and we'd all be up by seven the next day even though it was Saturday. Duncan and I would probably be up at six. Our kids love weekends and are eager to start enjoying them early.

The fact of my 6 A.M. wake-up call was rarely out of my mind as I moved through the evening. How late would people stay? Even if we managed to round things up by nine, we still wouldn't have time to get the kids to bed, clean up, chill out briefly, and get eight hours of sleep. Our children would be grossly underslept no matter what.

I'm deeply invested in Joseph and Ben getting enough sleep, partially because I'm obsessed with the pursuit of eight hours for myself. Eight hours is so precious, so rare, so beautiful that I can get resentful of anyone or anything that threatens to get between me and it. Invited guests? Get the hell out. Making love with my husband? Not so appealing if it cuts into my eight hours. A movie? What movie is worth so much? Sometimes I've even fantasized about going back in time and forgoing a few of the dumb all-nighters when I stayed up doing cocaine with people I didn't like or crying over the end of a relationship I see now (of course I see it *now*) as botched from the outset. I'd love to reclaim those hours and trade them in for sleep chits. Sleep is my god.

We were operating at a pretty brisk pace the night of the potluck, and it seemed quite possible that I'd be able to squeeze in seven and a half hours of sleep. I hoped I wasn't herding people too obviously. By 6:05, we were already seated for dinner—adults at the dining room hand-me-down from my mother, kids just inches away at a plastic table I'd dragged in from the kitchen. The meal was salad brought by Thea, pasta and grilled chicken by us, and French bread and chocolate ice cream from Sarah and Connor. It was all palatable to kids, but not too plain for adults. I'd put out fancy plastic goblets for the kids to use, and one was promptly knocked over. Sarah rushed to deal with the situation. "So sorry," she said, wiping with her napkin.

"No problem," I said, "this is a fully spilled-on house."

"Hey, there's apple juice on my pasta!" Thea and Rick's six-year-old son, Reece, yelled. He started poking the spirals with his spoon. It made a *gluck-gluck* sound.

"Gross!" Joseph shouted, and mad giggling erupted all around.

By 6:20, the kids had finished eating and were playing fort in the bedroom, just behind the dining room. They'd taken the sheets and blankets off the bed and made a canopy using chairs. All the stuffed animals, about three dozen, were in the fort as were hundreds of tiny Lego pieces. The Legos were candy that the animals were madly trying to eat. "They just broke the piñata!" I heard Joseph explain.

The kids were having a great time, and everyone from barely three-year-old Ryan to seven-year-old Cynthia was included. The situation made me really happy. It was possible, of course, that everything would explode in a fury of tears and violence at any second. On the other hand, our small group may have passed some critical developmental milestone. With two three-year-olds, a four-year-old, two six-year-olds, and a seven-year-old, it finally seemed unlikely that anyone would bite anyone else or poop on the floor. I loved hearing my sons happily engaged with the other children (would that they grew up to be less anti-social than I am), and I felt a thrill of anticipation about the new conversational world that may have opened up for us adults. At 6:45 with the kids still self-ticking brilliantly in their fort, it appeared that we might not be interrupted at all. Where would our talk go?

It dove directly into the past. Connor started off, describing the students he'd taught in Argentina, then moving on to the salads he'd eaten. "Every day, I ate a beautiful mesclun salad," he said, "in the courtyard behind my apartment in the hacienda."

Duncan, who'd lived in Greece for two years, chimed in. He, too, had taught English and eaten many wonderful salads—by the sea, no less. He'd drunk a lot of retsina, a wine made from pine trees, and traveled all over Europe and Africa, going up the Nile once on a small sailing boat with two obnoxious German women. Connor offered several more nuggets from his life in Argentina, and I felt myself growing keen to say something about my own adventurous past. I didn't want my guests to view me as simply a mom, someone conscientious enough to serve organic peas to her children, but without a lot else going on. Did they think I'd always lived this outwardly conventional life: a house, a husband, two kids? I had also done exciting things! I wanted people to know that men like Duncan and Connor weren't the only ones who'd been exploratory.

Plus I was irritated that two men were dominating the conversation. Connor may have started us off, but I held Duncan to a higher standard. I could see that he was trying to help in a way, to turn a monologue at least into a dialogue, but I was still pissed. How often had I been at a table of four or six where two men spoke 80 percent of the words? How many other people, just in the city of Austin, were experiencing the very same dynamic right then?

Thankfully, Thea jumped in with a story about a guy she had dated at Williams who turned out to be a professional pretender. He's famous now for posing as a prison guard, a blind man, and a pimp, then writing books about each of his experiences. "He was a jerk," Thea said, "but very compelling."

This led me to describe, after a somewhat strained segue, the Rush concert I'd attended in New Orleans with a warlock I'd dated briefly and the way he'd whispered the pagan messages he was intuiting from the lyrics into my ear. I didn't say I went to the concert because I was lonely and miserable, or because I felt compelled to do something real since my near-constant daydreaming about a fictive man and child by the sea was starting to frighten me. I did admit to not liking the guy, finding the music horrendous, and never believing—even for an instant—that Rush had any deep, hidden agenda. Still, I was aware as I was speaking that I was romanticizing the evening, the sheer fact of its occurrence. When, in my current life, would I make time to do something as irrational, inefficient, and random as going to a bad concert with a warlock?

Soon everyone was offering up funny and crazy anecdotes from their pasts, even Rick and Sarah, who were the most taciturn of the group. The conversation grew extremely animated, and our guests' faces lit up in a way I had never seen, certainly not as we raced past one another to pick up our kids from preschool. The stress I'd thought was permanently lodged in our thirty-something brows seemed to be on vacation. I, for one, was thoroughly enjoying myself, so much so that I forgot to keep checking my watch. And the children were still buzzing happily behind us. Was this what people meant by sociability and good cheer? How could I have forgotten? Had things truly been so different just a few months prior when some of us still had two-year-olds, or had I been wrong, unnecessarily misanthropic, to have dreaded precisely this kind of social event for six long years?

I was truly happy that evening, and yet I also felt sad that the stories making our faces brighten were all solidly rooted in the past. Of course sharing stories about your past is a primary way of getting to know people beyond the surface—in our cases, beyond the harried day-to-day hustle of life with young kids. I was glad and eager for our backward-glancing talk for that reason. On the other hand, weren't our current lives funny and interesting? Didn't we do anything adventurous or carefree now?

Apparently not. We were laughing at our foolish, younger selves, but it was also clear that we mourned the loss of their footloose ways. Still, I felt certain that none of us would trade what we had now for what we had then. Even if more were possible, verbally reminiscing about the past was as far as any of us wanted to go.

For myself, I realized clearly that I actually had what I could only dream of at twenty-three. While love without an inordinate cost to the self wasn't all that was necessary for a rich and full life, it was nothing to take lightly either. It was a gift I had worked toward and also been given by Duncan, Joseph, and Benjamin. So what if our house was dirty and not on the sea? I had blessings to count. I promised myself I would count them. More important, I would attempt to sit with the people I loved, as well as a bunch of other folks, without counting anything.

I owed this attentiveness to my earlier self. She had been better at sitting than I was, and this was part of why I missed her. Above all, each of us at the dinner table missed ourselves with time to spare. Time vs. love, love vs. self—the brilliant thing about a fantasy is that these conflicts don't have to exist. It's all possible at the same time, in the same room, so long as the script is written entirely by one dreamer. I'm still quite fond of my paella-by-the-sea fantasy of life with a preternaturally quiet child and a gourmet man, yet I also see it as a chilly, controlled vision. In real life, where nothing is guaranteed or predictable, moments of transcendence happen even as some shout, some scrabble for pretend candy, some initially talk more than others, and some pine for the past. If this is life with others, I choose it over the dream. In terms of motherhood, I chose and continue to choose it with joy. At the same time, I feel compelled to speak up when I see something damaging to mothers, particularly if it seems insisted on by our culture. The enormity of this task first struck me during pregnancy.

TWO

A Pregnant Self

*When I found out I was pregnant the first time, I set up a dry-*erase board in our kitchen and kept track of every single thing I ate or drank. *What to Eat When You're Expecting* was my bible, and the commandments it laid down were challenging. I made a color-coded chart of all the nutrients I was supposed to ingest each day: 4 servings of protein, 2 of vitamin C, 4 of calcium, whole grains—4–5 servings, 2 high-fat sources, 2 iron-rich sources, 2 green leafy vegetables, 1–2 yellow vegetables or fruits, 2–3 other vegetables or fruits, plus at least 64 ounces of pure, bottled water.

Foods not to eat—if I'd felt compelled to write those out—would have taken up at least a school-sized chalkboard. Even a pregnancy idiot like myself—an idiot at the beginning, before I started reading—knew about alcohol, drugs, and tobacco. But who knew that bacon, or any cured or smoked meat, converts in your stomach to nitrosamines, which cause cancer? Or that all fish that swim or spawn in lakes and rivers (trout, perch, whitefish, carp, sea bass, and East Coast salmon) are off-limits to pregnant women due to possible contamination by

PCBs? That swordfish contains high levels of methylmercury; caffeine causes birth defects; decaf is created via methylene chloride, a carcinogen; and that gentle herbal tea—in those boxes with soothing New Age sayings—can cause diarrhea, vomiting, heart palpitations, and miscarriage?

Granted, there are many well-informed, environmentally savvy folk who know all this before, or regardless of, pregnancy. For me, though, the world suddenly became a terrifying place. Poisons were everywhere, and I had to be vigilant 24/7 to give my child the best shot at exiting my body unscathed. Avoiding the bad, and buying, cooking, and eating the best, right things, then checking them off on my board, was pretty much a full-time pursuit. And I had considerable help from Duncan, who shopped, cooked, charted, and worried along with me.

There's a woman with too much time on her hands, you might be thinking. Indeed I had been laid off from my job a few weeks before I got pregnant. I collected unemployment during my first trimester, which I preferred to think of as "pregnancy wages." At each weekly visit with my job officer, I fantasized about answering truthfully when she asked what I'd done that week. "I grew ten toes," I imagined saying.

I was proud of myself, my body, for doing what I could only view as miraculous work. I'd never been athletic or able to dance. What had my body ever done before, other than pee, have sex, and walk around? Growing a baby was amazing. I was amazing. And I was determined to do everything just right. For the first three months—before I was back at work—I basically spent all my time eating, napping, doing pregnant yoga and pregnant aerobics, and reading every pregnancy book I could get my hands on.

One afternoon as I lay in bed, surrounded by pregnancy books, I began to cry. I was taking such good, albeit obsessive, care of myself. Why hadn't I been able to do this before—or even some minor, modified version of it—when there had been only me? Could my actions be motivated by love—love for a cluster of cells I'd never seen? If so, how could I possibly love this cluster more than myself, whom I'd known and been with every minute for thirty years?

There was a particularly stark difference between how I was treating myself and my fetus now, and how I had acted at my most recent job, director of The National Abortion Rights Action League of North Carolina. At NARAL-NC, I routinely worked seventy- and eighty-hour weeks, sometimes lobbying at the absurd hour of 4 A.M. when the pro-life forces would attempt to tack abortion restrictions onto unrelated bills and slide them past tired, absent, or less committed pro-choice legislators. I spent a lot of early-morning hours racing around the General Assembly building, waking up Democrats and corralling them back to the chambers to vote.

Other people at NARAL (all women, with the exception of one man, our secretary) worked as hard as I did. The work ethic we championed was martyred and self-righteous. We were saving women's lives, we couldn't afford to have outside lives ourselves. It was competitive—who could be more dedicated, more effective, more exhausted—and the atmosphere felt incredibly gendered to me, like the collective modus operandi was definitely one that women would have thought up. It reminds me of the way I often see mothers acting: making huge personal sacrifices for the sake of another person, or persons, who are seen as infinitely more important, and needy, than the self.

While at NARAL, I never exercised, rarely got enough sleep, and ate lots of junk food, shoveled in from Styrofoam boxes. I developed stress-related medical conditions—ovarian cysts and keratoconus, a degeneration of the cornea. Often in my life if I've been too blind or stubborn to recognize that a certain situation isn't good for me, my body will start sending messages—louder and louder until they become impossible to ignore. This was one such time, and I started to get angry. I was twenty-nine years old, too young for stress-related illnesses. And how about the irony of NARAL as a pro-choice organization? There was no way in hell someone could work at NARAL and "choose" to have a baby. The staff were all in our twenties, all single, most of us chain-smoking workaholics. Some of the board members had children, but they didn't have to make the daily commitment we did.

I started to want out, and I started to want a baby. An overwhelming urge to become pregnant seemed to sweep over me all of a sudden, inexplicably. Duncan noted that it seemed particularly intense around 6 P.M., just as darkness came on. "Stop looking at me like that!" he'd say. "I'm more than sperm."

"Sperm, sperm," I'd mumble as I walked toward him in fake robot style. "I—must—have—sperm."

What was up? I couldn't figure it out. I was in love

with Duncan, I knew I wanted to have children with him, but why did I want a baby so suddenly, and right then? Was this what people meant by a biological clock ticking? Mine seemed a tad early.

I wonder now if part of my desire to become pregnant at that moment was because I couldn't imagine a balanced, healthy life just for me. I don't think I could have let myself live the way I did as a pregnant person—eating well, napping, exercising—if there had been only me; it would have seemed lazy and selfish. Wanting a healthier life was definitely not the only—or main—reason I got pregnant, but now that I was, couldn't I view pregnancy as an opportunity to take good care of myself without guilt, and feel happy about it?

I was crying that day on my bed because I wasn't sure. It seemed so sad that I needed an unquestionable, socially acceptable reason beyond myself to eat well and exercise. An innocent life affixed to my own, not just guilty old me. This way of thinking terrifies me because it's suspiciously like what I see as the crux of the pro-life movement's belief system: The fetus is innocent, whereas the woman—who has sex, who wants things for herself like a job, money, respect, and self-determination—is guilty, guilty, guilty. Pro-lifers, at least the angry ones I encountered firsthand, seem to hate women who have the power and self-worth to act on desires of their own. They see war between helpless fetuses and evil, selfish women. This makes me furious, and it's why I've spent significant amounts of my life in the pro-choice movement. Yet what the pro-lifers spout is what many women, pro-choice activists included, feel inside, at least during our bad moments: *What I want for myself, as a self, is selfish and bad. What counts is what I want, or should want, for others, especially husband and children.* Perhaps this is why the pro-lifers are so dangerous—this and their penchant for bombing.

How had these fetal evangelists, who used to send me death threats on a regular basis, gotten inside my head? What was wrong with me? I knew better than to believe this woman-must-be-selfless crap. My ambivalence about self-care didn't originate with the pro-life movement, though; it's part and parcel of what it means to grow up female in this culture. The denial of self for the sake of others was in full force in the NARAL office itself, after all. Is this pressure present, to some degree, wherever women go?

NARAL wasn't the first place I'd overworked. In graduate school, in other jobs, as an undergrad, as a high school student, I'd pushed myself very hard at times. My motives had never been entirely other-defined. Desire for approval, desire to surpass gender-stereotyped expectations, low self-esteem, genuine interest in what I was doing, a sense that it was important to "give back" to the community, and ambition are some of the forces I've felt pushing me.

By thirty, I was tired. The way I'd been living my life was exhausting. Maybe I'd always wanted a justification for taking it easy. As a pregnant person, I had one. Could I relax now?

I was napping, but I was also studying nutrition and pregnancy books like there was some big exam coming, and the stakes were higher than ever. Pregnant, I was somewhat of a maniac and a perfectionist—that much was consistent with who I'd always been. But wasn't this different? If my field of study was my body, my health, perhaps this signaled some kind of positive shift. While it might take pregnancy to make me learn the ways of self-care, wasn't there hope that I'd be able to continue them afterward, when I wasn't pregnant?

Here's the snafu in that plan: Pregnancy, and only with a first child, is somewhat of an anomaly in terms of the mothering experience. It's the one time when what's healthy for you—enough sleep, good food, exercise—is also unquestionably good for the baby. While most of the baby books try to convince you that a mother's and child's needs are basically consonant, I didn't find this to be true, especially not with an infant. Too often I saw my needs in direct competition with my infant's. I could either breast-feed or eat. Sleep or comfort my child. Forget exercise, leisure, relaxation—they didn't even make it into the game. It wasn't much of a game, really, since the baby's needs nearly always won out. After all, he was cute, "innocent," and weighed only fifteen pounds. And there I was with filthy hair, more than a tad of rage, a past of mistakes and guilt, and twenty pounds of postpartum fat. Whose need to eat should come first?

Once when my sister-in-law was visiting with her two-month-old before Duncan and I had kids, she shut the door on her wailing and recently fed daughter so she could eat dinner. I didn't know whether to be impressed or horrified. "For once, I'm going to sit and have a meal," she said.

Was this good, possibly feminist? Or was it callous, destined to create an insecure child? I knew nothing about babies at the time, and without a child of my own or much contact with other people's children, I was still able to admit my ignorance. This is the last time I can remember not having a quick and immediate judgment about something I saw another parent do. Within two years, I was a mother myself and smack in the land of continual judgment—my own and other people's.

I'd judged myself and others before pregnancy—it just hadn't been constant. In fact, the way I scrutinized everything I ate while pregnant was both new and incredibly familiar. Like every middle-class white American woman I know, I'd been through episodes of keeping meticulous track of all the food that entered my body. I would count every calorie I consumed and subtract any I later threw up. I wasn't bulimic, per se, but I drank heavily at times, and sometimes I would puke. I didn't plan to throw up, but if I did, I counted it as a dieting bonus.

At fifteen and with my mother's urging, I took prescription diet pills, ate little but carrots, celery, and cheese, and lost thirty pounds in three months. In my mid-twenties, I became macrobiotic for about a year. For some, macrobiotics can be a step toward health, but I was primarily attracted to the prescribed extremism. By eating a very narrow diet, I developed intolerance to a wide variety of foods—tomatoes, most fruits, dairy, wheat, corn, and all nuts. While I doubt if this is related to macrobiotics, I also became temporarily unable to swallow if eating in public.

Right before I got pregnant, I went on a detoxifying

diet and ingested nothing but grapefruit juice and vita-mins for five days; grapefruit juice, vitamins, and rhubarb for the next five days; grapefruit juice, vitamins, rhubarb, and an oily cut of sea bass for the next five days—on and on, adding only one new and bizarre food each five days for six months.

Watching what we eat—like hawks—is a way of life for many girls and women, much of the time. (Thirty-nine percent of American girls in grades five through eight say they're dieting.)* My goal as a pregnant woman—health, or at least a healthy baby—was new, certainly in its wholehearted manifestation. My goals previously had included self-punishment, control, and attractiveness. But viewing my body as something to be watched, restricted, and tightly managed was nothing new at all.

One of the most extraordinary sections in *What to Eat When You're Expecting* is called "Selections for Selective Cheating." The authors give two lists, preceded by these instructions: "Cheat no more than once a week with no more than one serving of the following." The second list is the more dangerous "cheat no more than once a month" list. Foods on the two cheat sheets include: a bagel or English muffin; waffles with fruit-only preserves; frozen yogurt with nuts, raisins, wheat germ, or fresh fruit; pretzels; 2–3 homemade oatmeal, date, or fig cook-ies; and a refined bran muffin.

Now, cheating, in my book, means snarfing three packs of Ring Dings. And there can't be rules for cheating

---

* Barbara Kantrowitz and Pat Wingert, "The Truth About Tweens," *Newsweek,* October 18, 1999, p.62.

because cheating means *breaking rules*. Cheating, in terms of food, is when you eat something really bad for you that tastes really good. Think of the sexual analogy: Cheating is hot sex with someone you're not married to. A lukewarm handshake with a dippy man you're not even attracted to isn't cheating; it's a waste of time, or worse.

According to *What to Eat*, having a cup of peppermint tea isn't even "selective cheating," it's strictly *verboten*. *Quick, someone come lock me up—I'm drinking herbal tea! Haul me off for child abuse!*

These books are absolutely maddening. And I read every single one I could find. I eventually stopped reading them in bed because they made me so anxious, I couldn't sleep. But I read them voraciously at other times, desperate to correct my pregnancy ignorance. I'm not sure how critical I was of them at the time, other than recognizing that they were anxiety-provoking. Now, I see them as bordering on evil. The books do contain some useful information. What's evil is their tone. And like the intense food monitoring I did while pregnant, the tone struck me as both new and incredibly familiar.

The voice used in most pregnancy and baby books is a twin to the voice of women's magazines—friendly, appearing to empathize, yet relentlessly goading you on to deeper and deeper, or more trivial and more trivial, levels of self-scrutiny. Like a best girlfriend, some would say. Not any girlfriend I want to have.

Are my thighs thin enough? Is my baby urinating enough? Have I mastered the best fellatio technique? Do I know the best breathing methods for labor? You will self-destruct, through implosion, if you live in a world of women's advice literature. First, you'll get a warning sign: a complete inability to stop asking, "What's wrong with me?"

I thought I'd figured out women's magazines, but I was oh-so-susceptible to pregnancy literature. I thought the food advice in *What to Eat When You're Expecting* was entirely different, say, from the Suzanne Somers diet as excerpted in *Glamour* because its goal was so much more noble than nonflabby thighs, because it was written by a nurse. But if the tone is identical, how different can the two really be? In a way, pregnant eating was the ultimate diet—the one I'd been practicing for all my girlhood years.

Pregnancy was also my introduction to the profoundly public nature of motherhood. At no other time in my life have strangers, acquaintances, and intimates offered me more advice. If you want to test this premise, go into a crowded bar eight months pregnant and loudly order a shot of tequila. See what happens. See if you feel like you're in a "free country." While pregnant women may feel free to take good care of themselves in ways they haven't before, as I did, they are unlikely to feel much latitude at all to do things that fall into the realm of even mildly self-destructive. Definitely not in public and probably not alone either.

Are you even alone as a pregnant person? The wife of one of my husband's friends once said to me, "I love pregnancy because you're never alone." Shit, I thought, she's right! And I *like* being alone. I *want* to be alone. Not always, but a significant part of the day.

Wouldn't it be great if I could alternate days of pregnancy with Duncan? If the choices had been (would that any of these were actually choices) I do the whole pregnancy or he does it, I would have picked me—at least for one of our children—because pregnancy was an experience I didn't want to miss. I viewed it, and still do, as something significant and desirable in itself, not only because of the baby that is likely to be delivered at the end. How extraordinary to hold another life inside my body! To be myself, and more than myself, at the same time. Now this was *amazing*.

And yet there were times when I felt like less than myself, the self it seemed I'd worked really hard to create. These were the times when I wanted to hand the belly over to Duncan for a while.

It wasn't a given that I would grow up to be a rugged individual, even a toned-down, partial one. My family and small Virginia hometown were fairly traditional. The women I saw growing up didn't do things on their own—not by choice anyway. Everything they did seemed interruptible. In fact, the women of my childhood struck me as always hoping someone would drop in, come home, relieve them of their aloneness. I didn't want a life like this. I wanted to be alone sometimes, to be able to concentrate, to write.

From age fourteen to thirty, it felt like I wrested a self out of places and groups of people who didn't always want me to do this, to be this. Lots of times I'd go somewhere like NARAL, thinking it would be a great place to hone myself, a feminist bastion, and it was. But it also encouraged self-denial in a way that worked against the creation of self. Where exactly can a woman go and experience total encouragement to blossom into her fullest, richest self? I'm still looking for this place.

I imagine—though I don't know for sure—that some people don't need to go anywhere, that they feel entitled to a self from day one, wherever they go. If this is possible, I want to raise my children to feel like this. Perhaps it's more likely for Joseph and Ben since they're boys. I don't want them to be oblivious to others, uncaring, or incapable of functioning in relationship, but I want them to have a strong sense of self, a right to self-determination. This strikes me as a very American desire.

Pregnancy was upsetting at times for me because I wanted, sometimes, to feel like an individual. I hadn't been an individual for that long—I really didn't want to lose her. There's no perfect analogy for pregnancy, for what it's like to be yourself and simultaneously contain another potential self. To not have the bodily integrity that many of us have come to rely on. The closest I can get is to imagine constant penetration of an orifice.

Imagine having someone's penis inside you twenty-four hours a day for nine months. "This is great!" I might think for an hour or so, assuming I knew and liked the penis-owner. I have a fairly intense desire for intimacy. Inevitably, though—and I'd love to know exactly when this moment would come—I'd say, "Go away," or possibly, "Go the fuck away!"

Would it happen eight hours into the experiment? Fifteen? No way could I go longer than that. I might not be able to handle more than forty-five minutes. It's weird to have somebody else inside you. While pregnancy doesn't always have to be in the forefront of your mind as having a penis constantly inside you surely would entail, pregnancy is a state that stops you from being able to view your body as simply you, as if your bodily choices will affect only yourself.

Of course, the notion of every person as an island is always at least partially a myth, as long as you live in relation to others. If I weren't pregnant, and I got sick or drunk, it would affect Duncan, at least mildly, if he were in town. If something more serious happened—a car accident, say—it would affect my friends, family, and co-workers. But with the small details of body management, adults—at least those without full-time responsibility for young children—usually have a fairly wide berth. Is there really any impact on anyone else if a nonpregnant woman has Twinkies for lunch instead of broiled chicken and a salad?

Not taking good care of yourself because you don't think you deserve it doesn't exactly indicate freedom. On the other hand, feeling unable to ever do anything slack— something mildly, or not so mildly, bad for you—isn't the sign of a free person either. Pregnant women and mothers of young children probably have the least societal go-ahead for even minor self-destructive behavior. Their responsibility to "innocent" others, to use the rhetoric of the pro-life movement, is viewed as too important and all-encompassing.

When I was pregnant the first time, the only thing I read voraciously other than pregnancy books were Sylvia Plath's poems and journals. In part, this reading could be viewed as professional since I was about to begin an M.F.A. program in poetry. Plath is a gorgeous poet, and I was reading up for my new embarkment into graduate school. And yet there are many poets I could have chosen to read. Why Plath, in particular?

I'd gone through an earlier period of Plath obsession at twenty. My boyfriend at the time began the extremely irritating habit of calling me "Sylvia" whenever he thought I was getting too morose or too angry. "All right, *Sylvia*," he'd say or, "That's enough, *Sylvia*."

To me, Sylvia Plath was the quintessential nasty girl, the poet who refused to act right or say nice, pretty, controlled things. And she was screwed over by her husband, Ted Hughes, who left her and their two young children to live with another woman. Hughes was also a poet, and in my estimation, a much lesser one. "Shut up, *Ted*," "You're acting like an asshole, *Ted*," I took to responding to my boyfriend, Alec, whenever he called me Sylvia.

By twenty-one, my interest in Sylvia Plath, and in Alec, had died down. Maybe I didn't need her anymore after he was gone. I needed her again when I was pregnant, though, that's for sure.

Pregnant, I was fixated on the tableau of Plath's death. I figured that as a poet she had constructed—visually and psychologically—exactly what she wanted to leave behind. The last action she took was to place her head in the oven and turn on the gas. This was coupled with her next-to-last action: placing mugs of milk and a plate of bread between her sleeping children, three-year-old Frieda and eighteen-month-old Nicholas. Maternal tenderness followed immediately by violence and self-destruction. How could someone enact such seemingly contradictory motions one after the other? "She was mentally ill," Duncan said, as Alec had also been keen on reminding me.

This answer didn't satisfy me. I was fascinated and terrified by what the connections between motherhood, poetry, and self-destruction might be; and what in specific, they might turn out to be for me.

In a way, I was banking on pregnancy and motherhood to wipe away my self-destructive urges, to initiate me into complete health. While I never viewed myself as extremely self-destructive (I always had company who seemed at least as messed up as I was), I did occasionally engage before pregnancy in unsafe sex, a variety of recreational drugs, overdrinking, binge eating, and riding with people who drove too fast. Sometimes I felt an urge to cut myself, but fortunately, I never did it.

By thirty, everything apparently had changed. I was eating perfectly and all organic. I was sleeping with one good man. I was carrying his child. We would create our own family—a new family, free and clear of the dysfunctions we came from.

This was a compelling narrative, and yet I kept reading Sylvia Plath. Motherhood hadn't cured her. Perhaps it had exacerbated what ailed her. It certainly hadn't made her into something other than what she had been before—a talented poet who was, occasionally, suicidal. While Plath's death was horrific and tragically early, it might have struck me as more horrific if she'd stopped writing as a mother. Plath didn't stop writing until the very end, and her poetry as a young mother was better than ever. This was encouraging. Her suicide was not.

What I wanted from pregnancy and motherhood was redemption from the behaviors I was sick of, and a kind of hands-off on the behaviors and traits I wanted to preserve. I wanted to tone down my self-destructive urges, but I didn't want to lose all sense of myself as a free agent. Free agents don't always choose well. Not having to is part of their freedom. I find it inaccurate, as well as condescending, to claim that when people drink too much, get high, have unsafe sex, overeat, undereat, overwork, or drive too fast, that their actions stem from "simple" self-destruction. I'd love to see a motivational pie chart for every dicey choice I've made. For example, SEX WITH ROY: 10% attraction, 10% desire for power, 30% self-destruction, 30% curiosity, 20% "kicks." Even if I could see how much of a particular choice should be chalked up to self-destruction, there'd be no way to peel off the self-destructive percentage and move ahead, or decide differently, without it. Self-destruction is packaged closely with other motives. And I'm not even convinced that self-destruction in itself is always bad, always something to be repressed or worked against.

I'm fascinated by what Jane Mead's poem "After Detox" has to say about the self-destructive urge. Here's an excerpt:

I can never explain . . . why I began
in the northwest quadrant of my forehead,
just above the hairline, and carved, with mother's
dullest knife, the long diagonal line that ends
at the right side of my jaw. Or how the wide red scar
—its shiny translucent skin—turned out
exactly as I wanted. I can never explain,

but it should speak for itself—the map
of a vision, proof that I exist. It's only honest—
*to wear your skin as if it were your own.** *

It is honest to wear your skin as if it were your own.
Where is the self located? In this case, is she inside,
directing her skin to make visible the scarred nature she
feels is most honestly herself?

Your skin is not your own entirely when you're pregnant, nor later when you become a mother. Others have
too intense a claim on it. Perhaps Jane Mead's speaker
cuts her face with mother's knife because mother is the
one who teaches her daughter, through her own example, to cut her self down. A strong-willed self who wants
to do weird, unproductive, or selfishly self-destructive
things has no business being a mother. Since cutting in
"After Detox" is depicted primarily as a way of proclaiming the self, not erasing it, the daughter-speaker is the one
who has the right to do it, rather than her mother.
Mothers simply aren't allowed to self-assert in such sick
and disturbed ways.

There's plenty of self-destructive behavior, of course,
that is condoned or even encouraged for mothers, but
it's not the cut-yourself-with-a-knife variety. Mothers are
supposed to be selflessly self-destructive; they can breast-
feed all night, for example, at the expense of their own
sleep for years on end, and arguably depleting their
own calcium supplies, which they'll need later to ward

---

* Jane Mead, "After Detox," *The Lord and the General Din of the World*
(Louisville, Ky.: Sarabande, 1996), pp. 23–25.

off osteoporosis.* At least in the social circles I run in, mothers who sleep with their children and breast-feed for many years receive mostly praise for their nurturant behavior.

To my mind, much of expected maternal behavior can be viewed as self-destructive or self-abnegating. But let a mother do drugs or swipe at herself with a knife, and she's selfish, not maternal. The two kinds of self-destruction, when coming from a mother, play entirely differently to a wider audience.

While I've never cut myself, I have experienced long-term sleep deprivation. I know many people swear by the family bed, finding that parents and children both sleep better nestled alongside one another. But I'm a light sleeper, and my children are wrigglers. Because I haven't done it, I can't accurately predict what long-term co-sleeping would do for me. But if it permanently increased my level of exhaustion, even slightly, then the family bed would be definitely worse for me than a knife wound. And arguably worse than one night of cocaine—unless I did too much, and it killed me.

I don't know what a fair comparison between the two

---

* 1986 study found that women's loss of bone mass was directly related to the length of time they breast-fed, that the difference was significant at the wrist site, and that it could not be compensated for by taking dietary calcium supplements (G. M. Wardlaw and A. M. Pike, "The Effect of Lactation on Peak Adult Shaft and Ultra-distal Forearm Bone Mass in Women," *American Journal of Clinical Nutrition* 44 [1986]: 283–86). Several studies have confirmed the fact that calcium supplements cannot stop bone-loss during lactation; others have questioned this result. See Jules Law, "The Politics of Breastfeeding: Risk, Reproduction, and the Gendered Division of Labor," *Signs: Journal of Women in Culture and Society*, vol. 26, no. 2 (Winter 2000).

choices would be—maybe just one night of broken sleep with my children vs. one night of cocaine or one knife cut. In this case, I'd definitely go with my children. I'm a different person now, partially because of being a mother. Still, I'm angry that certain forms of self-destruction, or self-sacrifice, are simply considered par for the course during motherhood, whereas others are supposedly indicative of the utmost selfishness, and therefore taboo.

Of course mothers do commit acts of "selfish" self-destruction, acts that combine self-annihilation with self-expression as Plath's suicide did, but the cultural pressure not to is far more extreme on mothers than nonmothers. For me, a person who apparently feels much less compelled to "selfish" self-harm than Plath did, the transformation from a person who could choose to hurt myself to a person who could not happened, irrevocably, during my first pregnancy. It felt like a blessing and a loss. I couldn't figure a way to get one without the other.

THREE

A Birth of One's Own

There's nothing like the prospect of giving birth to bring up a woman's issues about control. There's a high likelihood that you'll be in extreme pain. What do you want to happen then? Someone to take the pain away, as effectively as possible, regardless of what has to be stuck into you? Or people not to mess with you, especially now that you're likely to be really stressed and frightened?

I didn't know. I thought I might want some kind of in-between. A team of midwives backed by a nonalarmist feminist doctor who would teach me breathing techniques, provide me with a Jacuzzi and herbal pain relievers, but then knock me out and wrench the baby out on their own if I couldn't handle the pain. If they did have to anesthetize me, I wanted them to compliment me profusely anyway, saying something like, "Good job! You handled a Herculean amount of pain; no one could have stood more."

I couldn't find any in-between option when I was pregnant the first time, and I looked high and low. I ended up planning homebirths with both of my sons, which strikes me, even now, as a fairly radical choice. For one, you basically forgo any possibility of pain relief if you give birth at home. I don't care if you're Herbal Sal or the queen of self-hypnosis; nothing less than an epidural truly cuts the pain of childbirth.

I'm no masochist, but I eventually figured—and I still stand by this reasoning—that people barking orders at me, or worse yet, just doing things to me, to my vagina, without telling me anything, would be worse for me than any physical pain. This was, basically, my view of the hospital. I'd never been a patient in a hospital, but I imagined it as a place where cocky men joked with one another while wielding sharp instruments. If you weren't docile enough, they'd cut you, out of spite.

I'd dated a medical student once, and he'd dumped me—partially, he said, out of stress. Even if he was a liar, medical school struck me as grueling and brutal. What if doctors never actually got over the experience? I didn't want someone with years-old unresolved anger attending me when I was in pain, my life or my child's possibly hanging by a thin thread.

I felt much more positive about midwives. I'd been very impressed by some midwives I'd interviewed in Mississippi when I was in college, and I'd even considered a career in midwifery. (A fear of blood stopped me from pursuing it.) Ideally, I would be attended by midwives in a birthing center, connected to a hospital. I wanted the midwives, but if I freaked or something went wrong, I wanted a doctor, preferably a skilled and emotionally adjusted one, to give me drugs and save our lives. But in 1994 in Austin, Texas, it was illegal for midwives to attend births anywhere other than home. My choices were homebirth with a midwife, or hospital birth with a doctor. No middle ground.

Ideologically, I much preferred the midwives' sense of birth as a partnership. With their sisterly help, I could birth my own baby. No one would deliver me of or from anything. Rhetorically, this sounded great.

Now, nearly six years after a failed homebirth with my second son, Ben, my thoughts are a bit different. After thirty hours of "unsuccessful," not to mention excruciating, labor at home, I ended up in the hospital attended by a non-condescending, highly skilled male gynecologist from South Africa and a white-haired anesthesiologist who looked just like my stereotyped idea of a patriarch, but who turned out to be kind, competent, and keenly concerned with my comfort at a time when this was exactly what I needed. And it was my midwife—my sisterly, good-at-listening birth advocate—who, after five hours of nearly pointless and murderously painful pushing at home, tried to talk me out of it when I said: "I can't do it. I want to go to the hospital."

And yet, if we have a third child, I might just try homebirth again. Duncan doesn't believe me. "How could you go back," he says, "now that you know what an epidural is like?"

I could go back—maybe—because physical pain, even thirty-plus hours worth, goes away. I'm angry that my midwife didn't take me at my word when my word contradicted her vision of how and where my birth should happen, and I realize now how ridiculous it is to assume that ego is solely a problem of doctors. But the thing I still have nightmares about is how Ben was wrested away from me in the hospital before I even had a glimpse of him, and how I felt utterly unable to ask for him because I, and he, were patients.

✳✳✳

What exactly do you sign on for in going to a hospital? I don't know one woman who has given birth in a hospital in the United States who doesn't feel that something unnecessary and disturbing—and in several cases, harmful—was done to her.

Is this enough reason to have a homebirth? Most women in the United States don't even consider it. Only 1 percent of American births happen at home, and some of those are by accident. Six months pregnant with my first child, I couldn't figure out what to do. I wanted to have a birth that felt like me. Me in a lot of pain, with a baby coming out, but still me. Was this too much to ask? Perhaps it was selfish. Nearly all the women who told me horror stories about what doctors had done to them in the hospital ended with the same coda: "But now I have my beautiful, healthy baby, and that's what really matters."

I certainly didn't want Joseph to die. He and I not dying was paramount. But did this priority mean we couldn't ask for anything beyond that? Was I tempting fate to want a positive birth experience *and* a healthy child? Why wasn't there a feminist birthing center in town, connected to an excellent hospital? Austin seemed to have a plethora of lefty choices in other areas of life: several vegan restaurants, two or three Green Parties, a thriving local ACLU. Both of my available birth options seemed so alien and frightening.

I decided to pursue both home and hospital birth for a while, until I could make a decision. I started home-birthing classes, but I also continued to interview doctors. Maybe I'd find one who was a midwife at heart, who had a secret room in the hospital not subject to the usual disempowering protocol.

✳✳✳

When Duncan and I showed up for our first homebirthing class, we were the only couple not sporting either some form of tie-dye or a crucifix. We never could have anticipated this. My mother, who was in town visiting, went with us that night. After class, she dubbed our classmates "interesting," which is her code word for "freaky as hell."

The mix of people was, indeed, really interesting. From what we could tell, two major groups seemed to choose homebirth, at least in Austin: hippies and fundamentalist Christians. Where should we even sit during class? Duncan and I aren't hippies. We own a house, eat meat, and drive a contemporary station wagon. And we definitely have differences with fundamentalist Christians. When I imagine a deity, it tends to be a warrior-She, kind of like Xena in the sky, but wiser and less quick to slash her enemies. At class that night, I said a little prayer of my own and sat down on an empty futon couch. Duncan sat beside me, his arm protectively around my shoulders. My mother sat in a nearby rocker.

I was anxious about homebirth, and my mother was *very* anxious about it. Since she was along that first night, I may have been even more prone than usual to hope for classmates who struck me, and my mother, as normal— i.e., like us. If there were lots of women like me planning homebirths, I figured it must be a responsible choice.

I'm not proud of my lumping, stereotyping behavior, and I've noticed that it comes on strongest when I'm worried or doubtful, as I was about choosing homebirth. I looked out at my classmates that night and saw a sea of hippies and fundamentalists. If Duncan and I weren't members of either group (and what disparate groups they seemed to be), then why, exactly, were we here?

Homebirth, so far as I could tell, was not an obvious feminist choice. None of my feminist friends had chosen it. If I could just spot another feminist in the room, I might feel better, safer, more at home. What do feminists even look like? I myself have medium-brown hair, and I dress in a style I'd call casual-slob. Maybe my classmates were hippie feminists and Christian feminists. If not a feminist, would an identifiable Virginian, writer, or ex–graduate student have assuaged some of my anxieties? My mother might have felt better if she'd spotted a few clearly professional women. It's stressful to feel like an odd duck.

Negotiating birth choices was my introduction to what has turned out to be a fairly constant sense of being weird and out-of-step as a mother. I'm speaking of a discomfort beyond the usual person-as-individual trying to function as part of a group. There's always been a bit of a rub there for me, as for most people I know. But groups of mothers and mothers-to-be strike me as different, or at least more extreme, than other groups I've been in. For one, the stakes are *really* high. While it can be kind of cool or countercultural to be incompetent in other contexts, it's never cool to be a bad mother. This may be the one thing that widely divergent people will all agree on. The Junior League and La Leche League may define good motherhood differently, but members of both groups aim for their group's ideal definition. Or else they keep their mouths shut.

When I disagreed or thought I disagreed with something I heard in homebirthing class, I kept my mouth shut, and I'm not usually the closed-mouth type. I felt I didn't know enough about homebirth to object, and I felt peer pressure to buy into, or appear to buy into, what I was being told. In actuality, I hadn't made up my mind yet. Part of me deeply wanted to believe that my body had her own feminine intuition, that she knew how to birth a baby on her own if given the chance. Another part of me registered "New Age crap" when the midwife told us things like forming your lips into the shape of an "O," then moaning "Ohhhhhh" would send a message to your cervix to also make an "O." This way, you could direct your own dilation!

Homebirth takes a lot of self-confidence, a lot of body confidence. I didn't know if I had it. I didn't know if I *should* have it. False confidence can be stupid, unrealistic, and dangerous. Could my body really birth a baby at home with extremely skilled coaching but minimal technology? I didn't know. I kept telling myself to calm down, to remember that I was in homebirthing classes provisionally and for good reasons, or at least out of reasonable fears about the hospital. I'd be able to figure out, ultimately, if I belonged in a homebirth. For curiosity's sake, I also hoped I'd gain some insight into why the hippies and Christians had signed on.

My Goddess-leanings definitely seemed consonant with the midwives' beliefs and aesthetics. They had statues of pregnant goddesses all over the classroom. I wondered what the Christians made of these idols. Perhaps they chose to see them as human figures. Or maybe the Christian clients, like me, figured that while there would be points of disagreement with the midwives, homebirth was still more in keeping with their belief system than hospital birth.

From conversations I had with the midwives and from comments the Christians made in class, I began to see that they viewed birth as a spiritual experience that a secular hospital would be likely to destroy. Also, strange men had no business compromising a Christian wife's modesty by sticking their hands in her vagina, whatever the reason.

Hippies, from what I could tell, didn't want the hospital interfering with what was natural. They also believed birth was spiritual, but their vision of God differed from the Christian conception. God, or Goddess, was more of a nurturing yet powerful Mother Earth figure. The birthing mother was like a representation, a manifestation, of Mother Earth giving birth to the world.

Over time, I began to see that our birth class was made up of individuals (who would have known?) who were like me, in that they were influenced by a mix of ideologies they found compelling. If hippie and Christian views were prominent in our class, there were definite points of overlap, and I had something in common with both. I too believed birth, in the right context, could be a spiritual event. But, most important, I didn't want doctors, especially male doctors, high-handedly doing things to my body. Feminism was my primary ideology of choice, but just like the Christians, I felt that birth was no time for strange male hands to be inside my vagina.

In terms of my overlap with the hippie perspective, we both chose to see God as female, although my God wasn't particularly maternal. She was more kick-ass and Amazonian. Only after birth did I realize just how kick-ass you have to be to push a baby out of your body. During my birth classes, I was sometimes annoyed at the gentle, earthy, peace-loving Goddess the hippies seemed prone to evoke. And I don't really believe in "the natural," per se. I tend to view just about everything, including childbirth wherever it takes place, as heavily influenced by culture. But I bonded with the hippies, as I had with the Christians, in not wanting doctors to mess with me. I might not be sure yet, or ever, about other parts of the justification for homebirth, but my wariness about hospitals and doctors was strong enough to keep me coming to class.

✳✳✳

I've had some bad experiences with doctors, but who hasn't? Nothing horrendous per se has happened to me, although the last time I purposely saw a male gynecologist was pretty bad.

I was nineteen and home from college for Christmas break. My mother had arranged an appointment for me with a gynecologist I'd never met, someone highly recommended by our heavily tanned dermatologist, Chuck Cartwright. My mother had dated Chuck in the 1950s before she met my father, and we all thought he was a swell guy. So I went to see Chuck's friend for my annual Pap smear. In the middle of the pelvic exam, Dr. Recommended-by-Chuck asked where I went to college. When I said, "Harvard," I swear he torqued up the metal speculum that was pinched around my cervix a notch tighter.

"Really," he replied icily. "I went to Mr. Jefferson's university."

As a born-and-bred Virginian, I knew that some inhabitants of my home state could be defensive about the University of Virginia. They could get downright angry if someone seemed to imply that going elsewhere might be a good option, especially a hoity-toity school "up north," of which Harvard is the most egregious example of all. Clearly, my doctor was this kind of Virginian, and he had me and my vagina pegged as wannabe-Yankee snobs.

As he continued to prod, swipe, and generally take way too long sticking things in me, he asked what I was doing while home on break. Stupidly, I told him: I was volunteering with the Virginians for the Ratification of ERA. I was young, a budding feminist, and nothing if not earnest. Passing the Equal Rights Amendment was one of the great feminist issues in 1982, as I perceived it.

The doctor smiled smugly, his hand still inside my body, and said, "Oh, come on now, women don't need the ERA. I know my wife doesn't. She's happy to let me make all the decisions."

Not that offensive of a comment, perhaps—God knows it could have been worse—but the gloved yet intimate context made it insufferable. I don't know that I thought of this visit at the time as a turning point, a final straw, but I managed to make appointments only with female gynecologists from then on.

The women gynecologists I saw over the next eleven years were more or less okay, although a few were definitely rude and arrogant, and I hated what I saw as their doctorly privilege and disrespect for my time. Once after sitting in the waiting room for an hour and a half, I was finally called back to the over-air-conditioned examining room to wait another hour, dressed in nothing but my paper "gown," with never so much as a word from anyone about the delay. By the time the doctor—a brusque German woman—finally got there, I was weeping from cold, anger, and the humiliation of wearing just paper for so long. This doctor was the only female gynecologist in Richmond in 1986, and she had a huge number of patients. It was either wait like that, or go to a man. So I waited.

When I got pregnant in 1994, I was living in Durham, North Carolina, and seeing a doctor I liked quite a lot— Dr. Wyatt. She was a feminist who regularly thanked me for the work I was doing at NARAL-NC. Our good-byes went something like this:

Me: "Thank you, Dr. Wyatt."

Dr. Wyatt: "No, thank *you*, Faulkner."

I never waited too long in Dr. Wyatt's office, largely because she told me when to come so I wouldn't have to. She did this, I think, because she saw me as a fellow professional, a busy woman who wore suits to my appointments rather than the drop-waisted denim jumpers of stay-at-home moms. She liked me and, more important, she respected me: We were two working women, committed to women's reproductive health.

It bothered me a bit to think that I might be receiving better treatment and shorter waits because of my job, but I certainly wasn't going to complain. I was busy, after all, and I didn't want to wait. I told myself that the women in jumpers might like sitting in the waiting room for hours on end, maybe it was a pleasant break from the kids they already had at home.

Because we moved to Austin when I was six months pregnant, I had to choose a new "caregiver." If we hadn't moved, I'm not sure how much investigation of birth options I would have done. I probably would have had my baby with Dr. Wyatt in a hospital, despite my negative view of hospitals. I certainly wouldn't have considered homebirth. It was illegal in North Carolina.

✳✳✳

In Austin, Duncan and I made appointments with two gynecologists—both women, both recommended by friends. The first was a high-heeled, long-nailed woman who seemed thoroughly disgusted by having to do pelvic exams. She did mine with a grimace in about ten seconds, then plucked off her glove, chucked it in the trash, and headed for the door.

"Is everything okay?" I cried after her, thinking perhaps I was a goner, and it was too horrible to tell.

"Fine," she muttered without looking at me and without slowing her rapid escape.

The other doctor seemed okay, but she was dressed in surgical scrubs, which I found unnerving; it made me think she was eager to operate. And even if I grew to like her a lot, it was pretty unlikely that she would actually be at my birth since she was in partnership with six other doctors. The doctor I chose would only be present—and probably just for the last few minutes when the baby was actually coming out—if my labor happened neatly between the weekday hours of nine and four-thirty, or if she was the one of six partners who happened to be on night-weekend call. This is common practice for most ob-gyns; it was Dr. Wyatt's protocol, too. Nevertheless, I didn't like it.

Call me picky, but I wanted to know without a doubt that the person I selected would be at my birth. And I wanted to know and feel comfortable in advance with the assistants or nurses she would have with her. The midwife whose homebirthing class we were attending assured me that, barring incapacitating illness, she would be there. And unlike a doctor who typically checks in with you a few times during labor, then shows up for the final five minutes, Samantha and her assistant (whom I could select beforehand) would come when I said I needed them, stay throughout my entire labor, and stay as long after the birth as was necessary. This protocol was quite comforting to me because I'm a nervous person. In my thinking, being in intense pain was no time to be alone in a hospital room or only with Duncan, who would be as likely to panic as I was; nor was it an opportune moment to be introduced to strangers.

Samantha would also make follow-up visits to our house one, two, three, and seven days after the birth. This also sat well with me. I knew nothing about babies or breast-feeding except what I was reading, and that was all abstract. What if I couldn't feed the baby or put his diaper on? Samantha would show us how and give us reminders until we caught on.

Interactions with a midwife are immediately different from those with a doctor. I called Samantha by her first name, as she did me. After we began working with her, she always greeted Duncan and me with a hug. During our appointments, which typically lasted an hour and a half (with no waiting beforehand), Samantha asked about our feelings about the baby, our sex life, and whether or not we felt "nurtured" by each other. This could have seemed like unwanted touchy-feely crap, but somehow it didn't. We were new in town, entirely without friends or family, and we needed Samantha's emotional support as much as we needed her skilled physical care. Maybe more.

When I arrived at my first appointment, Samantha

was wearing shorts, a T-shirt, and sandals like I was. I liked her casual style because it didn't remind me of illness as white medical coats tend to do. Her office was attached to the back of her house, behind a defunct cedar hot tub, and exams took place on a double bed covered in an Amish-looking quilt, with Goddess statues looking on from all available surfaces. The waiting room was bedecked with beanbag loungers, vibrant paintings of naked women squatting out their babies, and tons of books on midwifery and childbirth. I was used to pastel doctors' offices full of demure Monet reproductions of French women in hats, *Self* magazine, and promotional literature for Depo-Provera. Samantha had created a more laid-back and empowering ambience, I thought.

At first I worried a bit about sterility. Samantha's bathroom seemed slightly grungy, and the lubricating gel she used came from a big tube instead of individual packets. For an exam, you just took off your underwear and lay down on a "chuck" (an incontinence pad) spread over a section of the Amish quilt. There were no paper gowns. But their point was kind of questionable, I realized. What were the gowns supposed to do exactly—protect you from the germs on your own clothes?

The speculums were boiled in a big soup pot on Samantha's stove. I hoped this was enough. It had definitely unnerved me when I'd worked at Planned Parenthood in my twenties and we'd scrubbed speculums with Lemon Joy. (They, too, had gone on to be boiled in a pot.) Shouldn't we have been using a product with a word like *Bacitracin* on the label?

Going to a midwife is an education in what hospitals

and doctors do that is unnecessary, unsterile, and dangerous. I never knew, for example, that rubbing alcohol
doesn't do jack. Iodine is what you need to sterilize the
skin. I was all ears for what Samantha had to say about the
horrors and stupidities of the medical establishment. This
was a real point of convergence for all of her clients—hippies, Christians, feminists, and the rogue unaffiliated alike.

One of the deal-sealers in my eventual choice of
Samantha was the way she expected me to know, and
want to know, about my body. Dr. Wyatt never asked me
questions; she seemed to think I wouldn't have any perti-
nent information. How could I? I wasn't a gynecologist, I
didn't have access to or understanding of her primary
tools, things like blood tests and ultrasound. Samantha, on
the other hand, asked me lots of questions: When does the
baby move most? What foods are you craving? Can you
feel your uterus contracting when you have an orgasm?
She wrote down my answers, and then we talked about
what they meant. She also assumed I would want to know
everything about what she was doing during an exam.
When she asked if I'd ever seen my cervix, and I replied,
"Not since the eighties," she laughed and held a mirror so I
could see what it looked like, pregnant, in 1994.

Duncan and I left our first appointment with two hundred pages of photocopied material on topics like the history of midwifery, nutrition and exercise for pregnancy,
herbal remedies for common pregnancy discomforts, a
list of supplies needed for homebirth, and arguments
against circumcision and in favor of breast-feeding. While
this information was clearly opinionated, it was also rich
and interesting. Dr. Wyatt had given me one fifteen-page

pamphlet produced by Johnson & Johnson with a soft-lit cover photo of a glazy-eyed pregnant woman staring off into space. Pregnant women turn stupid—that's all I could gather from the photo. The prose seemed to support my interpretation; it was condescending and totally uninformative. I felt like the message on every page was, *Don't worry, don't think too much, trust your doctor.* It pissed me off. And I did worry. Lack of information always makes me worry more.

The wealth of reading materials Samantha offered (all of the books in her library were available for client use) and her encouragement of my questions translated for me into a sense of control over something that made me really nervous—being pregnant and giving birth. Control was too compelling to turn away from.

Yet I was afraid of the at-home part. What if something went wrong? Samantha gave us studies showing that lots of what goes wrong during childbirth is caused or exacerbated by the hospital. For patients with identical risk factors, rates of infant death, injury, and infection are all much lower for those who have midwife-attended births, especially homebirths, than they are for patients attended by doctors. Several studies show that even when midwives care for higher-risk patients, these women and their infants still have better results than lower-risk patients seen by doctors. Dozens of studies we read confirmed that rates of episiotomy and C-section are much lower when midwives are the primary birth attendants.*

---

* According to Lewis and Morgaine Madrona, "Every study that has compared midwives and obstetricians has found better outcomes for midwives for same-risk patients. In some studies, midwives actually served higher-risk populations than the physicians and still obtained

With Samantha's encouragement, it began to seem like common sense to me that the hospital isn't the greatest place to be if you're not sick. Lots of other people there are sick, and at least some of what they have is contagious. While pregnant, I read an article in *Mother Jones* about new strains of airborne bacteria that can't be killed by the cleaning products hospitals use. The article went on to say that secondary infections—infections people catch in the hospital—are the third leading cause of death in the United States. No way did I want my newborn drawing his first breath in a cesspool of germs.

Of course Joseph or I might need the hospital. Even an

---

lower mortalities and morbidities" (Lewis and Morgaine Madrona, "The Future of Midwifery in the United States," *National Association of Parents and Professionals for Safe Alternatives in Childbirth News*, Fall–Winter 1993, p. 30).

A six-year study done by the Texas Department of Health found the infant mortality rate for doctors in hospitals was 5.7 per 1,000 compared with a rate of 1.9 per 1,000 for nonnurse midwives at home and a rate of 1 per 1,000 for certified nurse midwives (Bernstein and Bryant, "Texas Lay Midwifery Program, Six Year Report, 1983–1989," Appendix VIIIf, Texas Department of Health, 1100 W. 49th Street, Austin, TX 78756–3199).

A matched population study comparing 1,046 homebirths with 1,046 hospital births found that 3.7 times as many babies born in the hospital required resuscitation, infection rates for newborns were four times higher in the hospital, and the incidence of respiratory distress among newborns was 17 times higher in the hospital than in the home (study by Dr. Lewis Mehl, published in 1977, cited in David Stewart, *The Five Standards of Safe Childbearing* [Marble Hill, Mo: National Association of Parents and Professionals for Safe Alternatives in Childbirth International Reproductions, 1981], pp. 247–53).

A study in New Mexico of 3,189 midwife-assisted births found an episiotomy rate of 5 percent and C-section rates varying from 2.2 percent to 8.1 percent. During the same time period, there was nearly routine use of episiotomies by physicians in many hospitals, and a C-section rate that varied from 15 percent to 25 percent (Sharon Bloyd-Peshkin, "Midwifery: Off to a Good Start," *Vegetarian Times*, December 1992, p. 69).

arguable control freak like me knew that some things are unpredictable. Duncan timed the door-to-door trip from our house to the hospital at five and a half minutes, and Samantha assured us that we could get emergency help as fast, if not faster, than someone who was already in the labor and delivery unit. Regularly admitted women in labor—at least in hospitals in Austin—have to sign a liability form agreeing that the hospital can take up to forty-five minutes to transfer them to emergency care. Coming from home in an emergency, I wouldn't have time to sign this form, and the lawsuit-fearing hospital would be more likely to deal with me immediately.

Perhaps most compelling to me in terms of safety was the fact that I believed Samantha was the best birth technician in town. She was incredibly experienced and well-respected, having delivered more than two thousand babies and never losing or injuring a baby or a mother. I had no faith in doctors—male or female—not to hurt the baby or me. I knew one woman whose infant was actually killed by a doctor's mistake, and I literally knew no one who would describe the care she received in the hospital as entirely, or even primarily, positive. One friend bled on and off for six months after the doctor ripped the placenta out, instead of waiting the usual five to ten minutes it takes for the placenta to begin coming out on its own, because he was leaving for a trip to the Caribbean. Another friend was given Pitocin to speed labor, then something else to slow it, something to speed it, something to slow it, ping-ponging back and forth for twenty hours, until she was finally told that labor "wasn't progressing" and she had to have a C-section.

Despite all the information on homebirth in general

and about Samantha in particular that I shipped up to my mother in Virginia, she said that her doctor friend told her—and she was just passing the information along to me—that homebirth was a dangerously selfish choice. *You* may be fine at home, she said, but what about the innocent baby? She didn't say, "innocent to your selfish feminist machinations to stay in almighty control," but I imagined her thinking it.

Was I focusing on myself before my baby in even considering homebirth? This is the big sin against which all mothers are judged, and judge ourselves. It's why we're quiet sometimes in the face of baby-related suggestions we disagree with. In terms of homebirth, I felt I had enough evidence that with the hospital as a nearby backup, homebirth was as safe, if not safer, than hospital birth for the baby himself. I quickly realized that the baby's health was the part of my decision-making I had to keep emphasizing in order to ward off criticism.

The health implications for my child did matter a lot to me; I certainly wasn't crazy enough to do something risky just so I could avoid the male-dominated medical establishment. On the other hand, I didn't really expect the hospital to kill my child if I opted for a hospital birth. I chose homebirth twice because I felt like *I* would come to less harm, feel more like myself, and be more empowered if I stayed home.

✳✳✳

There was, however, the issue of pain. When I was eight and a half months pregnant with Joseph and all set for a homebirth, one of Duncan's colleagues, Sandra, told me that she had been out of her mind with pain during her first birth. She had wanted to do everything naturally, "like we all do nowadays," she said, but the labor had been so excruciating that she'd essentially missed the entire experience. Thanks to the epidural she'd gotten with her second son, though, she'd been able to relax and be fully present for that birth. "Think hard about doing it naturally," she said, "you might just miss everything."

This made sense and scared me. Lots of pain might not be empowering; it could cause me to lose myself. What if I was so overcome by pain that I had no idea that this was one of the most important days of my life? What if I was so wrecked after the birth that I didn't care about, or possibly even notice, Joseph?

Sandra didn't make this connection, but I also wondered about the way her first son seemed troubled, and her second son sunny. Mothers are on trial from the very beginning: Had Sandra, perhaps, failed to bond with her first son because of her pain and exhaustion? Did he psychically pick up on her distress and blame himself, acting out forever after, trying desperately to recapture the maternal love he didn't feel in the first few crucial minutes?

It seemed unlikely, but who could say with certainty? Once during the months of Ben's babyhood when I was depressed, I went to a craniosacral masseuse who said she had to clear the trauma I'd experienced in my mother's birth canal from my skull. I was thirty-four years old. Could a bumpy trip out of my mother's body be what was wrong with me thirty-four years later? The masseuse thought so.

You never know exactly what will count, and how, when you're a mother. I felt compelled to make Joseph's birth as gentle on him as possible so he wouldn't be depressed years later. If I could hack it, this might mean birth without anesthesia. But if I couldn't, and I tried anyway, Joseph might have lasting psychic scars. Of course, I didn't know that either of these unhappy effects were inevitable, but neither did I know that they weren't. Pregnancy is a prime time for anxiety. If only I could know in advance how bad the pain was going to be, I'd be able to better predict whether I could hang in there without drugs. I was terrified of the pain, and I felt completely unprepared to handle it, despite the training I was getting from Samantha in breathing techniques. Breath, just *breath*—that's all I'd have to rely on?

When I told my sister, Celia, that I'd finally decided on a homebirth, her response was, "Oh, uh-huh," then silence.

"Uh-huh, what? What?" I demanded.

"Well, you haven't really had much experience with pain," Celia said.

"What do you mean?"

"Well, there was the time you turned a cartwheel in the house and hit your foot on the open drawer—that seemed to hurt a lot—and then the time you slit your finger by using the wrong edge of the scissors to make a ribbon curl, but the time I remember most was when your finger got pinched in your ring while we were at that fancy restaurant in Virginia Beach, and Uncle Phil had to pry it off with a fork. You really made a scene then."

Celia was right. I didn't have much to fall back on— no marathon running or mountain climbing, not even any minor falls resulting in broken bones. I'd never even had a sprain. In the only operation I'd ever had, the removal of my impacted wisdom teeth, I was high as a kite and feeling nothing but a bizarre form of paranoia from the Darvon I took. In fact, a bootleg refill of that Darvon prescription helped me make it through the very visceral pain of high school.

I grew up on drugs. In my house, people took prescription antihistamines at the first sniffle, liberal doses of Midol for any perceived cramp at any time during our menstrual cycles, and handfuls of megavitamins. My father ingested daily horse-sized antibiotics to control a strange and innocuous condition he called head goobs.

When two college friends visited me at my parents' home right after we'd all graduated, they stumbled on a kitchen cabinet chock-full of pills. "My God," they said. "Now we know where Faulkner gets her pill habit."

"That's nothing," my mother replied. "Those are just the pills for the dog," and then she matter-of-factly showed them three more cabinets full of human pills, and these were just the downstairs supply.

I came of age in the late '70s and '80s and basically partook of what those decades had to offer psychochemically—marijuana, hash, cocaine, mushrooms, LSD, quaaludes. I never felt particularly abnormal or troubled, since everyone around me was also doing drugs. Oddly, it's some of the same people who took lots of drugs in the '70s and '80s who seem most interested in drug-free labor now. At first this didn't make sense to me. As Bette Midler says, "Childbirth is a helluva time to give up drugs." Why were all these ex-druggies—and here I definitely overlapped somewhat with the hippies—suddenly planning to go drug-free?

Duncan, who did not take drugs in his youth, had this explanation: It's all about a desire to experience life intensely. The drugs most people took recreationally in the '70s and '80s have the effect of making life seem more intense, more of a rush, more surreal. During birth, the way to experience what's going on most intensely is to have no drugs at all since the ones that are offered lessen sensation rather than increase it.

This seemed like a plausible explanation to me of what other ex–drug experimenters might be doing. But for me, lack of access to drugs counted as a definite downside to homebirth. If an average day in high school could drive me to heavy painkillers, how would I possibly manage unmitigated childbirth? I didn't know, but it still seemed more doable than losing control as a patient in a hospital.

Pain relief or control strikes me as a real bummer of a choice to offer women. Shouldn't we be able to have both? American feminists worked hard in the 1970s to demedicalize birth, and one result is that women are not routinely anesthetized during labor. We also now have the option, at least in some states, of being attended by midwives who subscribe to unmedicated births. Yet how feminist is it to choose to experience excruciating pain? Of course, *to choose* is key. But does any woman who hasn't had a child know what she is choosing—either to experience or to avoid? Even if you have had a child, you have little idea of what your subsequent births will be like. I was certain that my second labor would be easier than my first—this was part of the reason I felt like I could stand to do it again without drugs. The first time, I simply had no idea what I was in for.

✳✳✳

When I woke up during my first pregnancy with contractions at 3 A.M., I called Samantha. The contractions were far apart—ten to twelve minutes—but I was scared and excited. Samantha congratulated me warmly, then told me to drink a glass of wine and go back to sleep. I did.

The next day, my due date, I felt fine. I decided to write Christmas cards. It was November, and I'd never written Christmas cards in my life. I didn't say on the cards, "I think I'm in labor, but it doesn't hurt yet" because that struck me as dumb and embarrassing. Instead, I wrote short upbeat messages like "So excited about the new baby!" I'd read every book there was on labor, and still, I didn't know if this was it.

I'd heard stories of women who felt no pain at all. One woman in my birth class had been watching a soap opera when the midwives arrived at her house. Her partner had called to ask if they could stop by since she was acting strange, periodically grunting like an animal. After about an hour of hanging out, Samantha finally convinced the woman to let them do an exam. She had been reluctant, apparently, because she didn't want to miss any of her show. When Samantha eventually felt for the cervix to see how dilated it was, she touched an ear. The woman was completely dilated and effaced, and she needed to push right away. Yet she had, at least consciously, felt nothing up to that point. I wanted to be that woman, but I was her unlucky twin.

About 5 P.M., true pain began. I was on the phone with my ex-therapist, just "checking in." I was too embarrassed to tell her I was in labor—or prelabor, as Samantha later clarified—because it seemed weird to be on the phone then. And I was supposed to have weaned myself from my therapist, who lived fifteen hundred miles away. About ten minutes into our conversation, a pain like the worst menstrual cramp I'd ever had multiplied by six hit me and took my breath away. "Good-bye," I said, "nice talking to you."

I called Duncan. He came home and made linguini. I ate some, threw up, and we decided to call Samantha. Contractions were coming every four to six minutes, and they hurt like what I then thought was a motherfucker. Surely I was about to have my baby any minute. Samantha's apprentice Peggy was there by six-thirty and did an exam. I was one centimeter dilated. None of the pain I'd had so far even counted. Labor begins when you're three centimeters dilated. Shit.

By 9 P.M., I was desperate. Surely I must be nine centimeters by now. Samantha had arrived, and she did an exam. One centimeter. "Maybe one and a quarter," she added. "I could do a cervical massage. It might help to get things moving."

"Do it," I said.

What she did brings new—and horrifying—meaning to the word *massage*. I think she basically yanked my cervix open. It hurt like an unadulterated motherfucker. I threw up instantly into a stainless steel bowl she had waiting.

"Don't call that a massage," I cried.

"I know it hurts," she said, and she stroked my head.

I did know that she knew. Samantha had six children,

and no painkillers during any of their births. I began to think she might not be human. How could she expect regular people like me to endure this kind of pain? Women give birth every minute of every day, I tried to remind myself. I tried to think of the Guatemalan women I'd seen on video in class squatting out their babies in seemingly effortless fashion while music that sounded like a cross between Brian Eno and the French national anthem played in the background. That movie was a big fat fake, I decided. Those must have been *other* women's babies—women who had died of pain offscreen—set down between pretend birthing women's legs. You can make anything look natural with trick photography.

"I don't think I can do this," I said.

"Yes, you can," Samantha said.

"You can," Duncan echoed, but he looked really nervous.

People say the pain of childbirth is some of the worst there is. Certainly it's the worst physical pain I've ever experienced, by a long shot. Like most women I know, except those who've been injured or are gravely ill, I wasn't used to physical pain. I wasn't even that familiar with long-lasting and strenuous physical exertion. Middle-class Americans in good health can typically live our lives in relative comfort—heat in the winter, air-conditioning in the summer. Physical exertion is usually voluntary and often artificial, perhaps even taking place on a StairMaster, NordicTrack, or step-aerobicizer. We can always step off when we've had enough.

You can't step off the pain of childbirth if you're at home. There's nothing to step into, except possibly something absurd like the three-hundred-gallon blow-up hot water tank we installed in our bedroom for my first labor. Samantha's apprentice Jade, who sidelined in renting hot water tubs, told me that a lot of the pain women feel during labor is actually fear and tension caused by being in the hospital. "If you can create a nurturing, soothing environment for yourself, a lot of the pain will melt away," she said.

Apparently hot water was a primary melting aid. But from my position crouched naked in the blow-up tub, I distinctly remember thinking, *I'm going to die of pain, right here in warm water.*

Perhaps the most absurd thing I heard from the midwives was that sometimes women have an orgasm during childbirth. Which women? Those who practice up by masturbating with a chain saw?

It's difficult to describe what labor pain is like. It's not like a knife stabbing you. It's definitely not something you forget so you'll keep wanting to have more babies. And for me, it bore no relation to intense menstrual cramps, except for that first contraction I had on the phone. In my opinion, to compare cramps to labor is like saying a pebble is Mount Rushmore. One positive thing I can say about my labor is that it got worse. What I mean is that I wasn't suddenly thrown flat on the floor by an unbelievable pain I could never endure. I had time to warm up to excruciating pain—plenty of time.

The pain wasn't localized like a toothache or a burn; it was all over my body, coming in waves that began in my uterus but touched every inch of me before ebbing back down, leaving me to wait for the next one. Fighting the contractions made them worse, but I couldn't exactly relax into them, as more peaceful souls had advised. From

10 P.M. until 2:30 P.M. the next day, I had to concentrate with every bit of mental energy I had in order to get through every contraction. I stared at a candle, did the rhythmic breathing I'd learned, and chanted to myself: "Blue, blue candle," or "Strong, strong woman."

This surprised me—how mentally taxing labor was. I think intense concentration is a given if you forgo drugs. Or maybe this was just me. In labor, I used what I rely on for everything else in my life—my mind. A dancer or an athlete, someone in closer communication with her body, might describe how she dealt with the pain completely differently.

People often tell pregnant women that you have time to rest between contractions. In my first labor, I had contractions beginning every two minutes or less for sixteen hours. They typically lasted forty-five seconds. So in the best case, I had one minute and fifteen seconds of "rest" before being run over again with pain. Samantha advised trying to sleep between contractions, but who can sleep for seventy-five seconds at a stretch? It was more terrible than anything to be woken by a contraction. The only way I could manage the pain was to be completely focused on my candle and my breathing. And I couldn't get into that kind of hyper-attentive state if I was coming from sleep. Whenever I lost my focus, I would see my father's face, contorted into its most criticizing, belittling form. It was the face of failure, and I fought it like mad.

I had no idea how to focus at first. When Samantha got to our house, I was curled up in a ball, eyes closed, periodically screaming. Duncan was trying to remind me of our breathing exercises, but I would have none of that. I was in a different world. Samantha told me, though, her face inches from mine, that I couldn't get away, that I wouldn't want to, that I had to open my eyes and focus. She taught me how, breathing with me until I got it, lighting a candle so I'd have a focal point. When I refused to stop clutching Duncan, she made me realize, without ever saying anything like "buck up," that I had to figure out how to stand the pain and push hard enough to get the baby out on my own. I had strong support from Duncan, Peggy, and Samantha, but as I had said I wanted—before I knew how hard it would be—no one was going to deliver me of or from anything.

At a particularly bad moment around 4 A.M. Samantha said, "It's only pain," and I was surprisingly comforted. These words would have really pissed me off if I'd thought she was making light of what I was enduring. What she meant, though, was that nothing was wrong.

Childbirth is an entirely unique experience in that you feel intense pain, and nothing is necessarily wrong. In fact, the more it hurts, the better things might be moving. I'd never waited out pain or distress before. In the past if my body hurt in the slightest way, I'd pop some Motrin, Tylenol, or even Darvon. If my mind or spirit hurt, I might have a beer or eat some ice cream. Labor was a rite of passage for me most obviously because it made me a mother, but also because it moved me beyond the slackness and comfort I'd clung to before. It was my grand marathon.

Fortunately, my husband's colleague, Sandra, was wrong about what the pain would do to me. In general, I'm someone who has real problems "staying in the moment." I'm easily distracted, and I often make to-do lists in my head, no matter how engaging my present activity is. When I was on vacation recently at a gorgeous rock in the Texas

Hill Country, I started worrying about how I'd make it back to the beach in North Carolina—what planes would be involved, what beach chairs we'd need, where I might get a sunscreen that wouldn't make me itch. Why couldn't I simply enjoy what I was doing right then?

Because I had to concentrate so hard in labor, the twenty-two hours when I was giving birth to Joseph were the most focused, present hours of my life. Painkillers would have left my mind freer to wander. Without any, I and my mind had to stay put. It wasn't always a joyful place to be. Samantha told me near the end of labor, "It won't be long until you'll be holding your baby in your arms," and I remember thinking—and feeling guilty about it, *I don't care about the damn baby, I just want the pain to stop.*

The pain did stop, and I had a son. I couldn't believe that this tiny person was here, that his fingers, toes, ears were so beautiful and alive. I was proud of myself. Look what I'd done! We ate lasagna and drank champagne. All in all, it was a difficult and wonderful day.

✳✳✳

When I got pregnant two years later, it was not a given that we would have another homebirth. For one thing, our insurance had changed, and the new policy wouldn't cover homebirth, even though it's a lot cheaper than hospital birth.* Also I had run into one of Samantha's apprentices, Moon, at a La Leche League meeting six months

---

* An average uncomplicated vaginal birth costs 68 percent less in a home than in a hospital (Rondi E. Anderson and Daud A. Anderson, "The Cost-Effectiveness of Home Birth," *Journal of Nurse-Midwifery,* vol. 44, no. 1 [January–February 1999], pp. 30–35).

after Joseph's birth. She told me that all the apprentices had just quit, as had Samantha's partner of seventeen years, Denise. Moon said Samantha was an egomaniac who told the apprentices in their orientation, "I can do everything myself without any of you. You're only here because I want to teach."

Way to go in terms of validating your staff, I thought. Plus, I'd seen enough to know how much work the apprentices were doing and that it was essentially unpaid work. Samantha gave her apprentices $25 for each birth they attended and nothing at all for the time they spent seeing clients, teaching classes, and vacuuming the birth office. Nurses in a hospital, even orderlies, made far better wages. What's more, Moon told me the apprentices were basically keeping everything, including Samantha, running. They had to bring her bagels because she would forget to eat, pick up her kids at school, and forcibly tuck her in bed for naps. It didn't sound good.

I was struck by the irony of my sisterly choice being called an egomaniac by someone in a position to know. I knew ego wasn't limited to doctors or men, but I thought I'd be hedging my bets pretty well in terms of avoiding arrogance by choosing birth with a midwife. Now I wasn't so sure. Samantha had been magnificent at our birth, I had no complaints there. Maybe part of the reason she'd been so good had to do with her ego, her belief in her own skill. She'd been full of pride after checking my perineum (skin between the anus and vagina) after Joseph's birth. "Look at this, look at this!" she'd exclaimed as she beckoned Peggy over. "Not even the tiniest tear. Do you see what good coaching can do?" At the time, I took her comment as our joint reason for celebration; it certainly didn't strike me as an obnoxious brag.

Samantha had been an extraordinary coach, guiding me closely through an hour and twenty minutes of pushing with constantly varying directions—push as hard as you can, push at 50 percent, push gently, don't push at all. She'd helped me give birth squatting on the floor, and she'd coated Joseph's head with sterile olive oil as he began to crown. All of this was designed to decrease the likelihood of tearing. According to her detailed instructions, I'd also applied warm castor oil packs to my perineum nightly for the last six weeks of pregnancy, and she'd shown Duncan how to do perineal massage (another misuse of the word *massage,* in my opinion, since this intense stretching of the skin around the vagina really hurts), which he'd done faithfully every other night for the last month. It had been largely due to Samantha's skill and advice, I thought, that I had no stitches, no tearing, no hemorrhoids, and practically no pain at all after delivering an eight-pound baby.

While my lack of postpartum pain probably also involved luck, I chose to read it as a payoff for the intense pain I'd experienced in labor. A payoff for having chosen homebirth with Samantha. Still, I didn't doubt for a second anything Moon told me at the La Leche League meeting six months after Joseph's birth. Everything she said was a believable underside to what I knew of Samantha.

About a year after my conversation with Moon, I ran into Samantha at the grocery store and wondered if she was on drugs, she seemed so manic. Her words raced out of her mouth, and she kept looking around like she'd lost someone. She had on smudged black eyeliner that made her look like a rabid raccoon. She definitely didn't look like someone you'd want to be alone with in labor.

While never this bad, Samantha had seemed a bit hyper and distracted sometimes at our prenatal visits, and it had worried us then. If she ran on super-high all the time, surely she would burn out. What if her crash coincided with my first labor pains?

We'd been greatly reassured when we'd had an appointment with her partner, Denise, while Samantha was out of town at a conference. If Samantha had crashed while I was pregnant with Joseph, calm and highly skilled people would take over. But now that all her support people had quit, we felt nervous about planning a second birth with Samantha. A prima donna may be superb in concert, but the audience never sees how many underlings are working their asses off to create her success. Without them, her voice may be strained and erratic, or the show may not go on at all.

✳✳✳

After some debate, Duncan and I decided on a homebirth with Samantha's ex-partner, Denise, who had recently opened her own practice in an office attached to her house, just a few blocks from us. Denise had almost as much experience and reputation as Samantha, yet she seemed much more stable. She was attentive rather than distracted, and thorough without being alarmist. The apprentices she had scooped from Samantha's practice were two of my favorites, and we could afford $1,600— the inclusive fee for nine months of prenatal care, the birth, and six weeks of postpartum care—which we would have to pay out-of-pocket. It was settled. We would do another homebirth.

There might have been a bit of machisma in my decision to have a second homebirth: *I'm a homebirth veteran, I can take enormous pain, all I had was two Advil* after *the birth, let me at it again.* In some circles, it's embarrassing to admit that you've done anything other than natural childbirth. One of my neighbors said her cardiologist husband used to tease her with "You're the only woman in a ten-block radius who had an epidural." The radius he drew is the lefty, earthy neighborhood I live in: Austin's Hyde Park.

I liked people's awed response when they found out how long I'd been in labor the first time and that I'd had no pain relief. Giving birth to Joseph was unquestionably the hardest thing I'd ever done, and I wanted everyone to know about it. I would have liked a visible sign of how strong I'd been, something like a woman's badge of courage, a purple cervix. Instead, it felt like the world—meaning people in banks, doctors' offices, the drugstore—seemed to view me, suddenly, as powerless: the little mother who, judging from her ratty clothes, was out of the workforce, possibly forever; who probably divided her time between breast-feeding and baking. A mild, loving, and selfless creature. I felt like shouting at random condescending clerks: "Being mild and loving is not what moves an eight-pound baby out of your body!" I was angry that right after I'd done the hardest thing in my life, people seemed to see me as the softest. I felt I got respect from the world as a suit-wearing lobbyist for NARAL. I got nothing, it seemed—in terms of power—when I went around town holding the infant I had birthed.

Because being a mother felt surprisingly and abruptly disempowering in many ways, it was even more important to me that I plan an empowering second birth. This is, in fact, one of the arguments homebirth advocates often make: Motherhood is a challenge so it's important to start off feeling confident in your own strength. I also figured that homebirthers are more interested in, and more respectful of, the hard work that constitutes labor. A birth class of these folks would want to hear all my details, would be sufficiently impressed by my strength—unless I wussed out in some way.

✳✳✳

I felt my first labor pains with Benjamin at the swimming pool, the only outdoor place a huge pregnant woman would be in Austin in August. The pain was strong enough that I knew it was labor, but the contractions were infrequent—twelve to fifteen minutes apart. I went home and tried to nap, but I was too excited, plus I could only sleep for eleven to fourteen minutes at a time.

We decided to go to the grocery store. I was six days overdue and eating like a sumo wrestler. It was impossible to keep the fridge stocked. One of the most stressful aspects of labor, at least for those who favor control, is that you don't know when it will begin, and you want everything to be ready when it does. Adequate preparation—food, a clean house, sterile sheets, people on standby to help out—is even more important for a homebirth. My brother, Justin, had just left that morning to fly back to Boston after a week of waiting with us. There was a gap of two days before my sister could get there. Sure enough, that's when labor struck.

At 6 P.M., we called Denise and told her the contractions were happening, but not too strong yet. "Go to bed right now," she said. "I will too. Call me when anything changes."

We were in bed by eight, but I couldn't sleep much because I was timing contractions and wondering why I was off to such a slow start. Wasn't the baby supposed to pop out this time? That was the plan. Everyone had told me a second labor would be half the length of the first, or less. Half would leave me with a hefty nine hours of labor and two hours of painful prelabor. No picnic, but something I thought I could manage without drugs.

The contractions weren't that painful during the night (I *knew* what bad pain was), but things picked up a bit around 5 A.M. It wasn't so bad, though, that we couldn't wait until the barely respectable hour of six-thirty to call Denise and the baby-sitter we had lined up for Joseph.

Denise bustled in a half hour later and greeted us with a cheerful "Happy Birth Day!" Duncan and I looked at each other nervously. Surely this would be our birth day—it was only 7 A.M., after all, and yet we had doubts. Joseph's birth had been so long, and it was our only experience. What if my cervix was capable, but innately slow? *Please, God, let this one go faster,* I thought. And then a quick and crucial edit: *Just let everyone be healthy, and I'll take whatever you feel you have to dish out. If you can, though, go easy on me, okay?*

Denise did an exam, and I was three centimeters dilated, which meant that everything I'd experienced so far was officially prelabor. This was discouraging because it had hurt—not like a ton of bricks, and nothing like moving from one centimeter to three centimeters in Joseph's birth—but enough to keep me awake all night.

By noon, I was only at four and a half centimeters. Denise hooked me up to a breastpump and had me take doses of herbs: blue cohosh, black cohosh, and immortal every twenty minutes. The pump and herbs were supposed to increase my body's production of oxytocin, the hormone that causes contractions. I threw up several times from the herbs, and things started to get decidedly unpleasant. My contractions still weren't regular in interval or strength, though.

"Why not," I asked. "What's wrong?"

"Sometimes this just happens with older women," Denise's apprentice, Marcie, told me.

I was thirty-three. I asked myself how much sooner I could have started childbearing. I seemed too dysfunctional in my twenties. How ironic that my body may have been perfectly attuned to move me through an ideally calibrated release of contraction-producing hormones when I had the emotional maturity of a field mouse. At thirty-one, I'd had to have about a million contractions, but they were eventually strong enough to bring Joseph out. How much had my body aged since Joseph's birth? God knows I'd been utterly sleep deprived the entire time. How could I be in any shape to face a birth potentially more grueling and drawn out than Joseph's when I was two years and eight months more tired?

I didn't voice any of these concerns to Denise, Marcie, or Duncan. I was trying to be a trouper.

Denise sent Duncan and me out for a walk, hoping this might kick up my contractions. I wore a huge sun hat, and Duncan carried my organic Gatorade and herbal tinctures, which I had to keep taking every twenty minutes. Walking in Austin in August is pretty excruciating for anyone. For a woman in labor, it was true torture.

I stopped and sat on the curb for every contraction, breathing in rhythm with Duncan and hoping no neighbors would see. Even though my neighborhood is fairly countercultural, I'd never seen a woman in active labor walking the streets. Laboring women should be in the hospital—this is what I expected the majority view to be in any American neighborhood.

When we got back, Denise did another exam—five centimeters. I started to cry. "It's like last time, it's going to take forever," I sobbed.

"This is not Joseph's birth," Denise said. "It's not always good to have everything happen fast; it's harder on your body. Your body knows what it's doing. It will do it."

Finally, around 7 P.M., I got to seven centimeters, the beginning of transition, which is the most intense phase of labor, and Denise asked if I wanted her to break the membranes and hopefully speed my dilation. "Yes, yes!" I said. "I want the baby out tonight."

I was thinking of how horrifying it had been to be in intense labor with Joseph at 3 A.M. The dark had made everything seem more ominous, and I'd felt more alone, like I was the only one in the world working anywhere near that hard in the dead of the night.

"Just remember a half hour from now that you asked for this," Denise said, and then she used something that looked like a knitting needle to poke a hole in the amniotic sac. Almost immediately, I was in heavy pain like I remembered from Joseph's birth. By eight o'clock, I was at nine and a half centimeters, and Denise asked if I wanted to push. She thought pushing might speed the last half centimeter.

"Yes," I said.

I pushed like hell for the next five hours with no sustained downward movement by the baby. Denise coached me through every contraction, often using the mantra: "Push, push, harder than it hurts." She had me run back and forth between contractions and push in every possible position—squatting, lying on my back, standing, kneeling.

My clearest memories of these efforts are of the small poop I left on the floor and Denise's discreet request to Marcie to "get that, please." And of me squatting, pushing as hard as I could, my fists slammed down on Denise's blue-jeaned thighs, feeling no movement, and looking in her eyes, saying, "Help me, help me, please, help me." And the frightened look in her eyes, and her response, "I will, honey, I will."

To my mind, labor and birth is an incredibly intimate time. Not a time, I still don't think, for cold metal stirrups and intervention from strangers, if at all possible. I had carefully considered the odds here as well.

The rate of transfer to the hospital for homebirths is about 8 percent, though Denise calculated her own rate as closer to 4 percent. A 92 to 96 percent chance that I could birth entirely with the people I'd chosen struck me as good odds. Better than the chance that any doctor I chose would be the one on call. But a doctor would be able to handle both uncomplicated and complicated births. If I was lucky enough to get my doctor in labor, and something went wrong, I wouldn't have to be transferred to someone I didn't know.

After five hours of pushing, eighteen hours of labor, and fourteen hours of prelabor, I began to think longingly of strange doctors, especially anesthesiologists, and I said to Denise, my friend and birth partner, "I can't do it. I want to go to the hospital."

Her immediate response was: "Yes, you can! You have all the strength you need to deliver this baby. And let me tell you something, it's not going to be easy at the hospital. You'll have to wait around for at least two hours, and you'll still have to do the work."

I started to cry, and Denise hugged me. Then she and Marcie went downstairs to give Duncan and me some time alone to rest, she said.

Her last pep talk really bothered me. In general, pep talks are a critical part of being a good midwife. I must have received more than a hundred from Samantha during the course of Joseph's birth, and I received at least that many from Denise, and to largely good effect. The last one, though, struck me as more of a lecture. It made me feel that Denise wasn't listening to me, or that she thought I was speaking out of wimpiness or temporary lack of self-confidence.

I found out the next day that Denise had gone downstairs and immediately called the hospital. "She did exactly what you wanted," Duncan said. Fair enough. Am I nitpicking to have wanted her to tell me her plan? "I hear you, I'll call right now, then we can discuss the options" would have struck me entirely differently than the words she did deliver.

Denise told me later that because she didn't want to upset me, she didn't tell me we were going to the hospital until it was all set up. First she had to determine which doctor was on duty; some were notoriously hostile toward women who had tried to have homebirths. "They hate us for thinking we can compete with them, and they hate you for thinking you can ignore them," Denise had told our birth class. She had seen a doctor refuse a woman's plea for an epidural until after he'd delivered a lengthy lecture on the stupidity of homebirth, she'd heard another mutter "crazy hippie freaks" under his breath as he entered the exam room, and she felt strongly that unnecessary C-sections had been given a few times as "punishment."

Fortunately, a good obstetrician was on duty my night of need. Perhaps because Dr. Gula was South African, he was quite respectful toward midwives and had no problem with homebirth for uncomplicated deliveries. Denise still wasn't sure we should give up and go to the hospital, though. Peggy, the apprentice from Joseph's birth, was in the kitchen as Denise and Marcie discussed whether or not to go to the hospital. We'd originally asked Peggy to come and video Ben's birth. For the past five hours, though, she'd been working side by side with Denise and Marcie.

Peggy told me later what she'd said to Denise in the kitchen: "Joseph's birth was really hard, and Faulkner never said 'I want to go to the hospital.' I think something's wrong." I wonder now if Peggy's words, rather than mine, were what ultimately convinced Denise that we needed to go.

After Denise came back upstairs, Duncan said, with more directness than is customary for him, "I don't want anyone's ego to keep us from doing what's best for Faulkner." Were his words the decisive ones?

Denise asked me to push one more time in the Taylor position (a modified lying-on-the-back pose), then said, "That's it. We're going to the hospital," and we were off in her SUV. She told me later that when she saw how completely swollen and distended my urethra was, she knew I couldn't push anymore.

From postbirth conversations I've had with friends, I've gathered that it's common to replay segments of a difficult birth over and over in your mind: *Why, exactly, did that happen? Did someone screw up? Could I have done anything differently to change things?* It's a quintessential "what's wrong with me, what's wrong with this" kind of moment. Everyone I know who's had a complicated birth wonders how much of her distress was inevitable, how much was caused by the doctor or midwife, and how much she might have created herself. I've heard friends flip-flop back and forth, over and over—*there was nothing anyone could do, the doctor is an asshole, I should have been more forceful.*

One of the two segments from Benjamin's birth that I continued to replay in my mind for months afterward was the hour between when I said "I want to go to the hospital" and when we actually left the house. It's not that I think Denise endangered either of us by the delay. Benjamin's heart tones were strong and normal the whole time, possibly because he never moved far enough down in the birth canal to experience even minor compression. My urethra was swollen, but that certainly didn't constitute an emergency. The decision to go to the hospital, in our case, was about my exhaustion. I wanted it also to be about my eventual sense and intuition that the birth couldn't happen at home.

Samantha and Denise were the ones who'd taught me to trust this intuition, this "body knowledge." I'd been a feminist in my head since eighteen, but my body had lagged behind. It wasn't until my early thirties that Samantha and Denise, plus karate training, helped bring a sense of power and communicative intelligence to my physical self.

The night of Benjamin's birth, I wanted Denise to trust my words, which I believed were a direct translation of what my body was telling me, and take me straight to the hospital. But this desire, when I look at it now, is based on a fuller reliance on body knowledge than I myself buy. I don't think people always, or even often, have clarity about what's going on in their bodies. It's impossible for me to separate what I know now—that Benjamin was too big to be born at home—from what I may have known then.

✳✳✳

When we arrived at the hospital, I told the nurse who greeted us at the door what I'd been chanting nonstop in the car, what I'd even shouted at the hospital parking attendant as we raced by: "I want an epidural, I want an epidural, I want an epidural." The nurse patted me on the arm, plopped me in a wheelchair, and said, "Anesthesia is *here*, baby."

These were some of the best words I'd ever heard, right up there with Samantha's "It's only pain" two years and eight months before. If the nurse, Denise, or anyone else, had said, "It's only pain" this time, I would have screamed, "Okay, motherfucker, you do it, you take this pain and ride it for thirty-three hours. You do it."

There's a limit to what a person can stand. I probably would have sold my soul to the devil for an epidural. I hope I wouldn't have sold my baby. Thank God it wasn't called for.

The pain in the car and at the hospital before I got an epidural—about an hour in all—was so unbearable, I think, because I knew there was no point to it. It wasn't taking me anywhere. I felt an incredible urge to push, but Denise told me I absolutely could not, that pushing would make my cervix swell, and I'd be more likely to have a C-section. I had to pant like a dog, squeeze Duncan's hand, and use all my focus in every contraction not to push. This was much harder and more demoralizing than pushing had ever been. "Productive" pain, like that in a birth that is progressing, is hard enough. Pointless pain could nearly kill you.

The epidural, when it kicked in, was fabulous. "Welcome back," Denise said, and I was, suddenly, back in the world. Duncan, Marcie, Denise, and I chatted calmly for two hours while I was having massive contractions, augmented by the IV of Pitocin Dr. Gula put me on, and I felt nothing but a mild discomfort in my lower back, as if I needed to shift positions. Chatting about spring-fed rivers near Austin, *Seinfeld*, and guacamole recipes was so different from the intense focus I'd had during Joseph's birth. "Please, be quiet!" I'd snapped more than once at Samantha and Peggy during Joseph's birth if they so much as whispered within my earshot during a contraction.

This time, chatting felt great. It felt normal. I realized with amazement that people all over Austin had been talking and breathing calmly for the past thirty-four hours. Meanwhile, I was on a nearby but unreachable planet. Planet Pain.

✳✳✳

With the help of the epidural and the Pitocin, my cervix, which had swollen shut to eight centimeters, was back up to ten by 4 A.M., and Dr. Gula told me I could push. I pushed as hard as I could; Denise, Marcie, and Duncan pushed down on my stomach; and when Benjamin crowned, Dr. Gula attached a vacuum suction to his head and pulled. It was hard work, and the epidural had mostly worn off so it wasn't pain-free, but it took only fifteen minutes to get Benjamin out.

He was enormous. Denise said she had never been at a birth where the woman had to push as hard as she could, a doctor had to pull, and three people had to push as hard as they could on her stomach *after* the baby's head was out. She also said, "Faulkner, that baby never could have been born at home."

I took this comment as a kind effort to keep me from feeling like a homebirth failure. But I didn't feel like a failure right then. In fact, I distinctly remember my self-righteous and unspoken rejoinder: "Duh. That's why I said I couldn't do it."

Marcie, apparently, did feel like we'd failed, and she was quite depressed for several days after my birth. I didn't see how else we could have done it so I didn't register "failure," per se, or depression. But I was definitely upset—immediately and for months afterward—by the unnecessary ways in which Benjamin's hospital birth differed from Joseph's homebirth. Upset enough that if we have a third child, I think I would opt for homebirth again, with the important caveat of stating up front to my midwife "If I ever say 'hospital,' I want to hit the road."

When Joseph had been born, Samantha put him immediately on my stomach. He'd been bluish and not breathing right away, and Samantha had said forcefully, "Talk to him! Tell him you're glad he's here."

We had, but Joseph's first few minutes had been no laissez-faire love-in. He'd needed to start breathing, and fast. Everything Samantha had done struck me as quick-paced and professional: There was heavy suctioning, and he'd been given oxygen from a mask. Still, I'd held Joseph the whole time, and Duncan and I had talked to him in what we hoped were soothing, rather than anxious, tones.

As soon as Benjamin was born, by contrast, nurses whisked him away to a table on the far side of the room, beyond my sight. Couldn't they have held him up for a two-second glance from his mother? Why was the table, which was on wheels, so far from the delivery bed, which was also on wheels?

I heard that Benjamin was 10 lbs. and 2 oz. before I saw him. In what way was he so big? Was he freakish; was all the weight lumped in one place—his neck, say? Denise and Marcie tried to reassure me, telling me repeatedly that he was beautiful. But in what way? I wanted to see! I'm sure I must have said this. How forcefully did I ask to see my child? I know I didn't demand that he be brought to me. How could I even think something so selfish when everyone was rushing around, apparently doing what was necessary for the health of my infant?

It was clear to me afterward that there had been no emergency. Benjamin was chubby, but he was just fine. He was in much better shape, in fact, than Joseph had been at birth.

The ten minutes between when Benjamin was born and when I first saw him is the second segment of his birth that I've replayed in my mind. *Why was he taken away? Why couldn't the nurses and pediatrician have worked on him beside me? What could I have said to bring him closer?*

While Benjamin was on the far side of the room, nurses washed him, weighed him, and put a paper diaper on him. Not even the most cautious doctor could claim that any of this was medically necessary. Did they think I was afraid of being peed on? Of seeing blood and vernix (the white coating on a newborn's skin)? I wanted to see everything and right away!

Perhaps people who choose homebirth are less squeamish about blood, placentas, vernix, and amniotic fluid than the general population. Even if this is true, I can't believe that most mothers, no matter what their "birth plan" is, would prefer to have their child thoroughly washed and diapered before they even got a glimpse of him or her. On what basis was this deemed necessary?

I don't think a malicious or arrogant doctor or nurse kept Ben from me for the first ten minutes of his life; it was, apparently, just hospital policy as usual. Dr. Gula certainly didn't order the diaper and wash. Benjamin was entirely out of his jurisdiction as soon as he was born.

Instead, pediatricians I'd never seen before rushed in and took over while Dr. Gula turned his attention to me— helping deliver the placenta, then stitching up my sizable tear. As he stitched, he kept asking, "Does this hurt? Does this hurt? Tell me if I'm hurting you."

He was a genuinely nice man, and I found his question utterly absurd. Does it hurt to pluck an eyelash after someone's leg has been cut off? I wanted to see my baby, I'd been through hell to get him into the world, and I didn't care at all about any minor stitching pain.

Duncan went immediately with Benjamin to the far side of the room and began talking to him in a soothing voice. "You're going to be okay, you're going to be okay," he said softly. Then Duncan called over to me, "He knows my voice, he's turning to look right at me!"

I was greatly reassured by this news. Our son wouldn't feel alone with strangers in his first few minutes of extra-utero life. Still, I wanted to be there, too! Wasn't this a moment when all three of us should be together?

More than a year after Benjamin was born, I still cried every time I thought about his birth, about missing his first ten minutes. "You were robbed of an experience you'd had before," my mother said. "You knew what you missed—the first precious moments of your child's life."

She was right. I wonder if I would have felt so sad if I hadn't had a homebirth before. Maybe I could have comforted myself by thinking that the pediatricians and nurses were just doing what needs to be done when a baby is born. But I had had a very different experience; I knew that even a baby who isn't breathing can still be held by his mother while assistance is given. The rushing in at the last minute, the faraway placement of the table, the weighing and diapering, were done primarily for the hospital staff's convenience rather than Benjamin's safety, my peace of mind, or our mutual (I assume it was mutual) desire to be together after the abrupt separation that is birth.

Still, Benjamin's birth is by no means a hospital horror story. Many people would view it as a story about the miracles of technology and good obstetric care. I view it, partially, this way myself. Would one or both of us have died in the nineteenth century? I feel fortunate not to have to answer that question. And I'm extremely thankful for Dr. Gula, the nurses, the anesthesiologist, the hospital, and the inventors of the epidural, Pitocin, and the vacuum suction.

Even my ten-minute separation from Benjamin doesn't constitute what I would call a horror. It's certainly nothing like my mother-in-law's tale of waking up alone in a hospital room in 1959 and having no memory of what had happened. By touching her stomach, she deduced that she was no longer pregnant, but where was the baby? Was it even alive?

My experience overall in the hospital was much better than I'd expected. Absolutely none of my fears about surly treatment came true during labor. I felt like a crazed ideologue to have ever written off hospitals and doctors so unilaterally. Dr. Gula, the nurses, and the anesthesiologist were nothing but respectful, kind, and skilled. They listened attentively to my concerns—that I get an epidural right away, that I not have a C-section—and they carefully explained my options and their opinions at every point. No one railroaded me into anything.

It was after the birth when hospital policy felt cruel and unnecessary. *What could have been done differently so that I wouldn't have been separated from Benjamin? Why, exactly, does it matter?* These are the two questions I still ask myself.

✳✳✳

Between the ages of one and two, Benjamin went through a period of clearly preferring Duncan's care to mine. Joseph had never gone through anything like this. "It's just a phase," everyone said, "it will pass." And it did.

When I asked Duncan at the time why he thought Benjamin seemed more attached to him, he said, "You're gonna get mad, but I think it's because my voice is the first one he heard."

Damn right, I'm mad. Those ten minutes were *it*, the defining minutes, so precious and crucial that nine months of in utero connection, eight months of intensive breast-feeding, and at least two years of more time parenting him couldn't hold a candle to "the first big ten" he shared with Duncan? Could this possibly be true? I thought babies could hear in utero. Surely Benjamin must have heard my loud litany: "I want an epidural, I want an epidural. Damn it, I want an epidural!" I suppose those words were considerably less welcoming, though, than Duncan's "Hello, sweet boy. I'm your daddy."

In general, I think it's a really bad idea for a mother to assess her skill and worth as a mother based on how much her child seems to choose her over his father. A child who is strongly attached to his father is only a good thing, in my book, especially when the parents are aiming for egalitarian child-rearing. And yet my feelings were hurt—and I wondered what was wrong—when we had to rush sixteen-month-old Benjamin to the emergency room with croup, and he absolutely refused to let me hold him. Only Daddy could hold him when he was sicker than he's ever been.

It's in these moments of high stress and hurt feelings that I find myself most likely to go down unproductive and anxiety-filled alleys. As crazy as it might seem to pin the future of a relationship on what happens in the first few minutes after birth, I knew that an incredibly influential book, *Maternal-Infant Bonding*, does precisely this. Authors Marshall Klaus and John Kennell claim there is a "sensitive period" at birth when mothers and newborns are uniquely programmed to bond with each other. The doctors compared mother-infant pairs who experienced eye-to-eye and skin-to-skin contact immediately after birth with those who didn't, and concluded that the early contact pairs had closer relationships later.

"Bonding" has largely been discredited now, at least to the extent that the first few minutes after birth are considered a make-or-break period. Nevertheless, the importance of bonding was emphasized in every one of the baby books I read, and it was cited often in our home-birth classes as one more reason that homebirth is superior to hospital birth.

I wanted to see and hold Benjamin immediately after his birth for my own reasons, but the fact that I wasn't able to is more crushing if bonding has any credence at all. I think it probably doesn't. If I had to ascribe a cause to Benjamin's period of preferring his father to me, I'd say it's much more likely that Benjamin turned more intensely to Duncan because I got depressed while he was a baby, or that Duncan and Benjamin are more temperamentally matched, or that because Joseph is more jealous of me and my attention, Benjamin grew accustomed to choosing Duncan in order to avoid conflict. But, of course, I'll never know for sure.

A person could go crazy trying to figure out why a child—or a grown-up, for that matter—feels a certain way in a given moment. Those of us who've been in therapy may be especially prone to look for early childhood origins for everything. It doesn't get much earlier than the first ten minutes of life.

I'm glad to say that I haven't spent much time at all agonizing about those ten minutes recently. Ben and I have a strong relationship, and I feel less anxious about most things now that neither of my children is an utterly vulnerable baby anymore. Still, I've come to recognize myself since Ben's birth as a full-fledged member of the community of mothers, rather than an odd duck who parents and thinks with anything near calm independence. The stakes in motherhood are, indeed, really high. I don't ever want to do—or wait silently while something is done to me—a wrong and irrevocable thing, a thing that could compromise my relationship with my child, or worse yet, his health and well-being. The ten minutes after birth are simply a heightened version of any other ten minutes as a parent. You'll never know for sure what the consequences of many of your actions and inactions will be on your child. This uncertainty, and my anxiety about it, mark me clearly as a contemporary American mother.

FOUR

The Joint Project

It has always seemed reasonable to me—and desirable—that raising a child be a joint project if there are two parents. Certainly it should not, ideally, be a sparring match. Yet long before I had a child or even felt that I wanted one, I began arguing vigorously with my boyfriends about childcare, housework, and power. If I could whip myself up into a full-on anger fest when everything was basically theoretical, what kind of battleground would actual joint parenting with a man be? The prospect was so chilling and exhausting, that on many occasions throughout my teens and twenties I felt it would be ludicrous to even attempt it. So much better—and purer—to have a baby alone or in community with other women. But—and it was an enormous *but*—parenting with the right man, a princely man, might be something other than a constant power struggle. Perhaps I was a sucker, but I half-believed in the Cinderella story. My prince was the fantasy man who cooked paella while I worked. Until I found his real-life counterpart, I felt compelled to battle the relevant issues with the regular guys I hooked up with.

THE SKETCH

At seventeen, my then-boyfriend, Jake, drew a crude picture of us in a house. He gave me big, crazy hair and set me upstairs in an A-frame box with a chimney on the left, looking out from a window. Himself he placed in the yard beside a dog he'd labeled Rover. A lopsided bird dubbed Sweetie Pie perched on the steep roof, and a baby with a grotesquely large head and wild, scribbly hair identical to my own peered out from downstairs. "Junior" was scrawled over the baby.

I don't recall any particular impetus for this drawing; Jake was, basically, a tease. I still use a ratty paperback thesaurus with "Faulkner Fox loves LSD" (untrue) penned along the top edge, grace of Jake. His sketch of us gone nuclear was likely made in the same spirit—to get my attention and provoke me. He may even have chased me around with his eerie and simplistic drawing, bashing me over the head with it, shouting, "This will be our life!" Depending on my mood, I might have accepted the chase, giggling and saying, "Stop, stop," in a flirtatious voice, but if he didn't, in fact, stop, I would have surely moved on to a pointed rejoinder like, "Quit being a dickhead."

The sketch was hideous. Jake meant it that way, meant to be perceived as poking fun, joking around. He never wanted to be more vulnerable than I was, and the reverse was doubly true for me. So we went around together half-assed and ironical as much as we could. Still, we thought we loved each other. It was not lost on me that Jake's sketch did portray, however crudely and ambivalently, what straight couples tend to see as "the goal." If we loved each other, we would eventually end up in a house with a baby—this was simply where heterosexual love led, as Jake and I both understood it. I found it flattering that Jake wanted to go there with me, as well as horrifying. I chose to focus on the horrifying since this stance was more self-protective.

"Why are you in the yard? Are you just gonna drink beer out there? Am I actually locked upstairs like the crazy woman in *Jane Eyre*, or am I just doing shitloads of laundry while you drink? Maybe you're about to barbecue, but that doesn't really count as work since you love anything involving fire. Why is our baby so ugly?"

A string of questions and criticisms flew from my mouth. Jake knew me, of course, and would have expected such a response, which is at least part of the reason he handed me a cartoonish sketch rather than, say, a heartfelt poem.

He made his sketch during a summer week that we were spending at his parents' house while they were out of town. (My parents thought they were in town.) Our occupation of the Miller house was just as ambivalent as Jake's drawing. We wandered around reveling in certain aspects of playing man-and-woman-in-house while doing our best to desacralize others: We drank Sea Breezes out of tall glasses with limes etched on them in the garden room while listening to Van Morrison, we had sex in the familial pool, we smoked pot on the roof, then made four cans of Campbell's alphabet soup and slurped it down at the heavy dining room table. Nearly every action we took could be viewed as mimicry, rebellion, or some blotchy combination, but always a response to heterosexual family life as we perceived it. We were not unlike a pair of male dogs, alternately sniffing and peeing on segments of his parents' Darien, Connecticut, life. The thought of actually taking over their lives, however, would have made both of us run for the city, the commune, the convent and monastery, the traveling circus—anywhere to escape what we thought we saw.

Jake's father worked fourteen-hour days as a high-paid executive in a pharmaceutical company in New Jersey while his mother knit and volunteered at a children's hospital. At night, they ate frozen foods like Stouffer's lasagna while a tiny black-and-white TV, placed directly in front of Jake's father, played *The Andy Griffith Show*. No one said a word. If this was nuclear family life, we were way too in love to handle it. We certainly didn't want to be away from each other for fourteen hours at a stretch.

How strange that marriage and familyhood—the goal of heterosexual love—seemed to *separate* men and women, to make them do radically different things all day long. Only war seemed as divided. During the week that I was at Jake's house, he turned eighteen, and we got stoned and drove to the post office so he could register for the draft. We were, as we would have put it that day, deeply bummed. There could be a war, and Jake could be killed. But if there wasn't a war, and we got married, *I* might be the one to die—slowly, trapped in a house in the suburbs, slipping away as his mother seemed to be doing in her odd frumpy skirts and knee-high vinyl boots. Her voice was so mousy, you could barely hear her. As she talked, I found my eyes moving down to rest on the pale, vulnerable knees peeking out between skirt and boot.

Their dry, blue-lined skin terrified yet compelled me, seeming to point to a host of confinements and losses, the root of which I was determined to understand.

Had she simply no chutzpah? If so, was she born with none, or had it somehow been stripped from her? I really wanted to know what ailed Mrs. Miller—because I loved Jake and he loved his mother, because I was curious, because I needed to understand in order to assure that nothing similar could happen to me. Jake's mother was an extreme case, but literally every adult woman I knew in 1981 (with one exception—the sister of a woman I baby-sat for who had no husband or children and worked for the State Department) appeared to be brewing in some morass of disempowerment despite the wealth some of the husbands, like Mr. Miller, had amassed. Could I really hook up permanently with a man, have kids, and fare better? Certainly, there was no chance at all if I couldn't figure out what, exactly, was going on. Could a house itself, or a particular kind of house, make a woman mousy? A house wasn't even animate. If it was children who oppressed women, how did they do it, being so small? In the case of Jake's mother, the simplest explanation—and the one that Jake himself put forth—was that his father was an asshole, and everything bad derived from that fact. While the numbers were outrageously high, it was conceivable, I supposed, that every married woman I knew had married an asshole. If so, I might just be safe! I loved Jake; he was definitely irritating at times, but he wasn't a full-fledged asshole. Still, details in his sketch—him in the yard, me upstairs—made me nervous. Why hadn't he drawn us side by side?

As long as we camped out in his parents' house illicitly, playing at their life, then taking it back while the Rolling Stones thumped in the background, we could stay together and on par, more or less. The less came during sex when he was having orgasms and I was not. This was a big problem, and I certainly hoped it wouldn't be permanent. Provided we worked out the sex, we could be happy as lovers and independent people, much more so, it seemed, than as full-time inhabitants of the sketch or his parents' house. As I saw it, Jake's sketch and his parents' traditional marriage promised less love for both of us and less power for me.

For these reasons, I never would have done a nuclear drawing, however satirical, when I was seventeen. At age eight, I might have, but by seventeen, it was crystal clear to me that I had a lot to lose in situating myself in some kind of house-man-child scenario. A lot to lose even if I couldn't figure out who—or what—would spearhead the loss.

I couldn't buy the asshole theory 100 percent; the numbers were too high. And even if it were true, the knowledge wasn't entirely comforting since a perfectly decent guy like Jake could turn into an asshole once married or possibly *because* he married. Power breeds bad behavior, and domestic heterosexual coupling as I saw it literally everywhere I looked was women with less power than their husbands.

Not that the husbands were necessarily happy—Jake's father was manic, insomniac, plagued by a stomach ulcer, and acutely insecure about whether or not his clients liked him. Still, his lot seemed significantly better than that of his wife. I didn't want to work in a pharmaceutical company, but I *really* didn't want to knit, putter, and volunteer. I was way too ambitious. Considerably more ambitious, in fact, than Jake, who alleged to only want to get high, have sex with me, and learn to play guitar badly so long as it evoked Jimi Hendrix, even slightly. His laidback pothead persona was part bluff, though—he was on his way to UPenn in the fall. I was headed to Harvard. While we both nurtured a fuck-it-all attitude at times, we were also engaged in intense preparation for our future, a future of work and achievement as we both saw it. And it was clear to us that our respective college admissions marked me as the more driven one, a position no silly sketch was going to make me give up.

THE NEPHEW

Three years later, Jake and I had long parted ways, and I was a junior at Harvard living in a decrepit house in Somerville, Massachusetts, with my boyfriend, Alec, and two other men. The house was disgusting—no one ever cleaned. I would have preferred a cleaner place, but I wasn't going to do more than the men, nor was I going to organize the forces, create a chore wheel. It was much easier, and more desirable, to live in filth.

Cooking was also rare. My housemates seemed to exist entirely on chocolate milk and conversation. Alec did make pesto—his only dish—about once a week while I alleged that I could cook three things: popcorn, quiche, and zucchini, one or two of which I'd make about once a month.

My inability to cook was utter pretense. I'd prepared elaborate foods at fourteen: chicken and dumplings, bagels from scratch, beef bourguignonne. I made old-style meals my mother viewed as unnecessarily caloric and time consuming. What busy mother of three has time for gourmet-ship? Best to leave that to the stubborn teenage daughter, determined to distinguish herself from her mother in nearly every arena. If my mother cooked fish, rice, and broccoli in twenty minutes flat (exactly the meal I make most often now), at age fourteen, I would spend all Sunday afternoon using every pan in the house to make chicken cacciatore.

At twenty, though, I no longer lived with my mother, and my self-definition needs had shifted. It was time to reinvent myself as someone completely unfettered by and uninterested in the domestic arts, just like my male peers.

If a man initiated cooking, I would typically help out since my intent was not to be lazy, just to preclude any expectation that I would run the domestic show. When Alec and I house-sat for his sister, Carmen, while she, her husband, and their four-year-old were on vacation, we used her whole-food cookbooks to make real dinners with fresh ingredients in their sun-filled, designer kitchen. Alec orchestrated the meals, but I worked busily by his side as sous-chef. Later we ate by candlelight, took mid-night swims in Carmen and Bill's lake, and had sex in their marital bed. What would it be like to have a life like this? Maybe not so bad—from our two-week house sit-ters' perspective.

Alec and I weren't driven to be as oppositional to Car-men's domestic life as Jake and I had been three years earlier for several key reasons: We were slightly less ad-olescent, we were invited house sitters rather than illicit squatters, and a sister's house is far less loaded than a parents'. Nevertheless, we still found plenty of cause for argument during our stint on the idyllic Newton Lake.

"Carmen loves sex," Alec pointed out one evening, seemingly out of the blue. I recognized his remark immediately, though, as part of our ongoing debate about marriage. Alec knew I was afraid of losing sex (by twenty I was having orgasms) and power if I got married and had children, and he liked to play—or be—devil's advocate. "Yep, she and Bill still do it all the time, even with a kid," he continued. We were sitting on an overstuffed couch in the den, listening to Joan Armatrading.

"That's great," I said, "but how come Carmen's a nurse and Bill's a psychiatrist? What's up with that?"

"She's not just a nurse, she's a psychiatric nurse—it takes a lot more training—and it's not her fault. Dad pushed her toward nursing school. It never would have occurred to him that Carmen could be a doctor."

Alec's father was a doctor, his mother was a housewife, his two older sisters were nurses, and Alec himself was entering medical school in the fall. The inequity, the sexism, of his family members' respective careers pissed me off, and I told Alec so—again. The subject had come up countless times before.

"Would you lay off my family?" Alec said. "I can't help what they do."

"Okay, fine. We won't talk at all." I reached over and turned off the record, *Whatever's for Us*. It was way too mellow for the situation anyway. "Let's just watch TV and pretend we're married," I continued, "let's pretend you're a surgeon and I'm, like, a maid."

"Jesus Christ!" Alec said. "You're not going to be a maid. Why say something ridiculous like that? Your parents have paid way too much in tuition for you to be a maid."

Alec had a point, but it wasn't the comforting kind. I knew I was extremely privileged: With the help of a few small government loans, my parents had been able to afford Harvard's hefty tuition, and people were always telling me I could "do anything" once I graduated. Most days these facts made me feel both guilty and panicked. On good days, I analyzed privilege and threw myself into working for various forms of equity and social change. At worse moments, all I could see was how much less privileged I was than whoever my boyfriend was. I was at Harvard, all right, but it felt like I could slip out of step with my male peers at any time. I had to be endlessly argumentative, ever-competitive, and completely thorough in my avoidance of the domestic, except when a man was right beside me doing his share or more. This behavior didn't mark me as a lunatic, by any means. Every college-age person I knew was incredibly competitive, and all my women friends fought with their boyfriends. We had to, we had to straighten them out, get them to stop thinking of their fathers' lives. Times had changed, and boyfriends had better get with the times, or step off. That's what we women told one another.

Boyfriends, for their part, had their own set of expectations. With Alec, the knottiest for me came into play when we hung out with his nephew, Casey. Whether Bill or Carmen were around or whether Alec and I were baby-sitting, I felt certain that Alec was watching me closely with Casey, assessing my proto-maternal abilities. I wasn't at all sure at twenty whether I wanted to be a mother. I was sure, however, that I wanted to pass Alec's test. He drove me crazy sometimes, but I still wanted him to want me.

Mothering, as I saw it, required much more important and complex skills than cooking, skills I didn't want to seem incapable of. A woman may choose not to mother, but if she literally couldn't do the emotional work it entailed, then I thought (and imagined Alec thinking) there must be something wrong with her ability to love. Loving Alec himself wasn't nearly enough of a proving ground since my feelings toward him—or any boyfriend—were likely to be all mingled with lust, panic, need, fear of loneliness, inertia, competition, and other less-than-savory emotions. Maternal love, as I imagined it, was pure and selfless—the arena where women proved their loving ability while men stood by to see who would fail. To suss out a woman who wasn't yet a mother, a man need only watch her with any child. I was certain that Alec was watching me with Casey, and I really wanted to pass his test.

Unfortunately, Casey was what most people would call a brat. He whined constantly, threw fits, and hurled his body around the house on hyper-speed, striking whichever people or objects got in his way.

"Shrinks' kids are always a bit screwed up," Alec explained with the authority of someone solidly en route to medical school.

I smiled wanly. Who knew what was wrong with Casey? Whatever it was, I was determined to work around it. I tried relentlessly to engage Casey—to throw balls to him, to chat with him about his life, to talk over the pros and cons of each grotesque Disney figure on his pop-up musical arcade. While Casey made the task extraordinarily difficult, I knew exactly what I wanted Alec to see in me. It went like this:

I was not a kid expert. I had no plans for a career in early childhood development; I would never, in all likelihood, work in a home for orphans; I hadn't volunteered as a Big Sister; and while I had done it, I had despised baby-sitting as a teenager. Tragic and sexist as it was, work with children was low status, and I was aiming higher, professionally speaking. (It was unclear to me at that point where, exactly, I was aiming, but it was higher.) Put me with a child, though—my boyfriend's nephew, for example—and I would miraculously, *innately,* one could say, be able to deeply understand the child and draw him out. I wouldn't relate in a typical maternal fashion, using high-pitched voices, clucks, and other demeaning verbal gimmicks, but rather through a deeper, more psychological approach. My strategy was simply to listen closely and talk, as if the child were a pint-sized seminar participant.

I wanted to think of myself—and be seen by Alec—as a maternal diamond in the rough. Not someone who went around advertising or developing her ability with kids (that would be "showy"), but someone who possessed mothering abilities intrinsically, in an offhand, Bruce Willis–gone-intellectual sort of way. If Alec never figured out that I really could cook—and I planned to go to my death with that secret, if necessary—he could step up to the plate full-time, or we could order takeout forever. But if I couldn't relate to kids at all, I felt certain that my girlfriend quality rating, and my closely associated self-image, would go way down. It was important to me that I not take this dive.

THE HOURLY CHART

Four years later, I was spending the summer in Germany with my boyfriend, Leo. (Alec had left me for a nursing student soon after he got to medical school.) Leo and I would be going to separate graduate schools in the fall—Leo to business school at Stanford, me to a Ph.D. program at Yale—and we were in Germany because Leo had a job there. My teaching jobs in New Orleans had ended in June, and Leo, who was making good money as a junior management consultant, was subsidizing my nonworking summer months.

During the day, I studied German at the people's community school with other nonnative wives and girlfriends of German men. It was a surprisingly disempowering scenario, not unlike acute housewifery, as I imagined it. My new Italian and French friends and I didn't have access to working papers, we didn't speak the language of the outside world, and we were dependent for money on male partners, men we didn't see for long hours of the day. We were also incredibly embarrassed and guilty about any unhappiness we felt since we were in love, we lived in nice apartments, and we were experiencing an international life to the envy of some we'd left behind in our home countries.

This particular situation was just temporary for me, of course. While it was slated to take six long years to accomplish, I was embarking on a path to power, legitimacy, and middle-class job security in the United States in just a few months via graduate school. It felt like a strange gift to have a few months of financial and cultural dependency on a man—a flash-forward of something I now had firsthand information that I didn't want. I had always imagined this kind of dependence would feel bad, and it did.

It was a tense summer for Leo and me: We loved each other intensely, we were fighting a lot, and we would soon be living apart. We had tried to end up at the same graduate school, but neither of us had gotten into any schools near the other. And neither of us was willing to forgo or delay school in order to stay together. I wasn't sure whether this was a bad sign, meaning we didn't truly love each other after all, or a good sign, meaning we were well matched in terms of ambition and likely, therefore, to have an equitable relationship in the long run.

One of the stress-aggravating exercises we engaged in that summer was making hourly charts of what our daily life would be like if we had a baby. To my mind, it never added up. Leo thought he'd go to work at 8 A.M. and be home by 7:30 P.M. With these hours off-limits, where could we go in terms of building an equitable division of childcare? Eight to seven-thirty was slightly less than Leo was currently working, but he figured he could cut back a bit for fatherhood.

"That's still too much time at work," I said one Sunday morning as we sat in bed, me scribbling 7 A.M., 8 A.M., 9

A.M. down the left side of an index card, and "Faulkner's work" and "Leo's work" along the top edge. "Babies sleep a lot, you'd barely see your child."

"Well, I could scale back when the kid turned five and was more interesting," he joked.

What a concept! I certainly didn't have much affinity for babies myself. I thought caring for an infant would unquestionably constitute work—in the case of one's own child, unpaid work. A job would likely be much better. But a five-year-old, now she could be engaging. Casey had been a terror, but many other young children—from what I could tell from a distance—seemed not to be. Perhaps Leo and I could both work long days for five years, thereby maintaining equity with each other while jointly making enough money to scale back and tune in to our child when things were more interesting and less arduous.

Could parenting possibly work this way? I wasn't sure.

"Well, whatever we do, whatever has to happen—diapers, feeding, whatever all there is because I don't know and neither do you—we'd be doing it *together*. I'm not going to do more of the work because I'm the woman."

"Don't worry," Leo said, "we'll hire someone."

Case closed? He thought it was. How else would we both work long hours? I could see his reasoning, but I still felt pissed by his suggestion, and the cavalier way he delivered it. I wanted parenting and all the domestic work to be a *joint project*, not something we largely subcontracted out. Sure, we'd need some kind of daycare—we both planned to work hard outside the domestic realm—but he couldn't buy his way completely out of the domestic work. Not and stay with me.

I decided to say something less confrontational at first, opting instead for a position that afforded me some moral high ground. "We can't both be gone twelve hours of the day," I said. "Our child won't recognize us by age five."

"We'll have weekends," Leo returned.

"You travel most weekends."

"You can come with me, like you do now."

This did not strike me as a good plan. Sitting alone in a German hotel with an infant while Leo worked long hours? No way. No way at all. "What are you—nuts?" I said.

"Relax," Leo replied. He stroked the back of my hand, the one still clutching the pen I was using on the index cards. "We don't have a baby, and we love each other. We'll figure it out when the time comes."

I did not relax. I barely ever relaxed, certainly not around topics of gender equity. Plus by that time, Leo and I were having lots of problems—some related to gender equity and several not directly—and I was beginning to feel that we would have to break up. I was sad, unrelaxed, and unsure if we could stay together, but I still wanted to hash out the hypothetical childcare issues—in case we could stay together and also because I found our discussions interesting and important in their own right.

"Okay, so if your job pays better than mine, which it probably will," I began again, "that doesn't mean your work is more valuable than mine, that advising companies on how to lay people off is more important for society than writing or teaching students how to think critically."

"In the Western World, that is what it means," Leo said. "But we wouldn't have to think of it that way ourselves."

"So you wouldn't try to make me do more housework because I got paid less?"

"I wouldn't make you do anything. I don't make you do anything now, do I?"

"No, but I end up doing more. Like I do all the shopping because the stores close at six. You're never home by six."

"Stores are open all night in America."

"Okay, but babies need things all day and all night. If I'm home more than you, I'll be doing more."

"So don't be home."

"Why would I want to do that? Why would I want to avoid our baby?"

"So be home." He looked satisfied with his cleverness, his answer-for-everythingness.

"Where will you be?" I asked.

Leo sighed. "I'll be anywhere you want me to be."

I knew he actually meant it, on one level. He didn't want to break up—that would have to be initiated by me—and he knew these conversations were critically important to me. They were my version of the partner test. If Alec watched me with his nephew to assess my long-term potential, I subjected my boyfriends to fairly frequent lines of questioning about childcare and housework. Still, these were just conversations, and it was a lot easier to say something than to do it. Plus, I didn't want Leo to share the childcare because I said to, I wanted him to do it because he saw that it was fair and because he believed in the joint project. I realized, however, that I didn't trust him to share the work for any reason once we were married, say, and he wasn't so afraid of me leaving.

By September, we had broken up. There were several

reasons, and while I can't say if this particular reason in itself would have ended our relationship, I was extremely unhappy about his long-houred corporate plans. I felt I had seen what corporate demands did to dash any possibility of equitable parenting—Jake's father, my father, Leo's father; Leo himself if he continued at jobs like his current one could no more take a child to a 4 P.M. piano lesson than fly to the moon. Were piano lessons even necessary or desirable? If they were, I didn't want to be the only driver.

As I saw it, to marry a capitalist—or a doctor—was to take on the lion's share of domestic work or hire another woman to do it, regardless of what a male partner said he wanted to do and regardless of what he did, in fact, want. The company would eat you up day-by-day while keeping you coming back for more with promises of the trappings of power: stock options, business class tickets and hotels, fawning secretaries, company cars. I found capitalism appalling, even though I'd benefited from its proceeds all my life. Capitalism wasn't any more fair than women doing all the domestic work was fair, and I'd learned to view the two as intricately related while I was an undergrad. Leo didn't refute this linking; he was cynical about the way capitalism worked. He still wanted the spoils, though, and was determined to get them.

"You don't believe in anything beyond yourself," I'd say, "you don't believe in justice."

"Why should I?" he'd reply. "What have poor people ever done for me?"

I never could come up with an adequately persuasive answer. Can someone be argued into a concern for justice? It seemed unlikely with Leo.

Neither Jake, Alec, nor Leo was a feminist or an activist of any kind. I loved them, especially Leo, but I began to think that love wasn't enough—not on the homefront, in terms of making sure it was a fair and harmonious place to be, and not in the larger world where we were sure to encounter a morass of injustices, a small piece of which I felt driven to try and alleviate. As my relationship with Leo was ending, I focused on the paella man again, whom I saw clearly as a leftist organizer in his noncooking hours. Was such a man out there? I thought I'd keep my eyes peeled.

THE PRINCE

Duncan was an avowed feminist whom I met at a political meeting of graduate students trying to form a labor union. His plans to become an academic promised flexible hours and considerably less morally suspect terrain, in my opinion, than management consulting. Still, this was rather surface information. What kind of a person was he? Friends of mine who knew him offered rave reviews.

"Duncan is a gem," a lesbian feminist friend told me. "I only have two male friends I trust implicitly, and he's one of them."

"He and Meg have just broken up for good," a straight feminist friend relayed, "and she still thinks he's a great guy. You'd better move now, if you're interested."

Good men were hard to find, as all of my friends—feminist and other—agreed, and at twenty-seven, I no longer felt I had all the time in the world to look. In the past, I'd often been lackadaisical in deciding whom to date, lackadaisical and old-fashioned. If someone pursued me even slightly, I usually relented. Otherwise, I did little or nothing. A more proactive strategy seemed in order this time, and I went after Duncan with direction—up to the point of getting him out on a first date.

Beyond the arrangement of the first date, I realized I couldn't predict or control much, nor did I want to. Duncan and I might hate each other after all, or less extremely, simply not hit it off. I had no intention of trying to hook up with a man who might possess a laundry list of desirable qualities, but whom I didn't love. While that may well have to be the plan at age forty-five, and with a severely reduced list of qualities (I fancied myself a realist), at twenty-seven, I still felt I had room—and necessity—for love.

Good fortune was on my side, and Duncan and I fell in love, as well as discovering a slew of shared affinities that reached far beyond politics. Three years later, we were married, I was pregnant, and I was in joyful expectation of beginning the joint project with my feminist prince.

FREQUENT PARENTING MILES

Four years after that, I was alone in a garage in Austin, Texas, attached on both nipples to a high-powered breast pump, while a disturbingly conservative undergrad took care of six-month-old Ben, Joseph was in preschool around the corner, and Duncan was teaching at the university. Ben's baby-sitter came for four hours every weekday, which was a huge blessing of time on the one hand,

and not nearly enough on the other. Certainly there was no time to futz around. I was teaching poetry to college freshmen, writing articles for magazines, and trying to wrestle my recent M.F.A. thesis into a book of poems. I could do none of this—or anything else, for that matter— longer than three hours without stopping to breast-feed or pump. Thankfully, I could read while I pumped if I held the book on a chair in front of me with my foot. But despite the extraordinary no-hands photo that came with my Executive Lady Medela Breast Pump, I found it nigh impossible to write while pumping. The milk tended to go off-kilter and spill down my front if I didn't use both hands fairly constantly to keep the tubing straight.

Breast-feeding itself was easier and more pleasant. Yet I was paying someone so I could have a few hours alone to work, and hooking up to a machine still allowed me— more or less—to stay focused on my work in a way that going into the house and chatting with the baby-sitter would not.

That particular April morning, I wasn't reading as I pumped. Instead, I was making a list—between tube-straightening maneuvers—of all the hours that week when I'd had the children, or had the children and simul-taneously done housework, while Duncan did something else: work of his own, sleep, exercise, a lengthy phone call to a friend. I decided not to list the half-hour at hand since I was merely pumping for a child who was twenty-five yards away with a baby-sitter. No, this should count as *my* time, however contorted and bizarre my bodily actions were. Why was I wasting it on domestic charting? I had so little time to work; every minute counted. Still, I kept going, noting the hours I held down the homefront on the left, against Duncan's hours in charge on the right.

Damnit, there were a lot of hours when I was busting my ass as a parent single-handedly! Hours not reciprocated by Duncan. What had happened to our planned joint project? This was hardly the first time the question had crossed my mind. More accurately, it would have been about the 12,000th time—a calculation based on 10 times a day x 30 days a month x the 40 months since Duncan and I had become parents.

I wrote "Frequent Parenting Miles" at the top of the page because I planned to cash in on the hours I had single-handedly parented our children. I didn't know yet what I would do or where I would go, but I knew my hours of freedom would come out of Duncan's account. He *owed* me, I felt certain, and while the past could be debated since there was no record (Duncan admitted he'd done less than I had during Joseph's infancy but claimed to be doing 45 percent now, whereas I estimated his current contribution as closer to 30 percent), from now on there would be a written tally as evidence.

Truth be told, during my highest moments of resentment, I figured Duncan owed me the minute Joseph was born. Duncan had ejaculated—which hardly seemed arduous—and I took it from there. He did, however, make a series of delicious meals while I was pregnant. Nevertheless, for equity's sake, I figured Duncan should be doing 75 percent of the babycare during the first six months of Joseph's life to pay me back for pregnancy and labor. Then we could move on to a straight 50/50 split for the rest of our lives. This was without consideration for breast-feeding, though. Given that we both thought breast-feeding was a good idea and only I could do it, a fair deal might have been Duncan doing literally everything except breast-feeding for eight months, then doing 75 percent for an additional six months, and then we could shift into 50/50 for perpetuity. The calculations for two children—one infant and one toddler—would be decidedly more complex.

We hadn't actually done any calculations like this, much less followed them. For one thing, while I can't say that I "wanted" to wipe spit-up off the couch, I did want to do many of the elements of babycare and childcare. Not by myself and not 100 percent of the time, but I did want to experience everything. I even liked diapering—talking to Ben on his little terry cloth pad, setting the tiny space heater to warm his butt when he seemed cold, noting how his day's digestion was going, then doing a raspberry on his sweet tummy before whisking him off the table into a big, kissing embrace. And I never would have agreed to hand Joseph's care entirely over to Duncan for eight months while I breast-fed Ben. I loved my sons. I wanted to take care of them. I just wanted Duncan to match my efforts.

I felt somewhat ashamed that I was now charting every hour, in quarter-hour increments, of our respective domestic laboring, but I also felt self-righteous. Hadn't Duncan driven me to this?

I'd thought that if I hooked up with the right man, a feminist man, I'd be able to stop my relentless comparisons. More than anything, that's what I wanted from home life—peace, a break from competition, and people who were unilaterally on my side. Clearly, I'd been naïve. There was a lot of strife between Duncan and me, and it seemed to ratchet up after each child's birth. If you love someone *and* he's a feminist, and you create children together—in our case, through acts of love—shouldn't the groundwork for peace and generosity be laid? Perhaps Duncan was a fake feminist, an armchair spouter of equity-talk. Or did the problem lie more with me?

Within two months of Joseph's birth, I was counting— or bean counting, as Duncan called it—all the time. On a day when Duncan was even home from the university, what was he doing while I breast-fed—something that, while appearing sedentary and peaceful, actually voraciously sucked energy out of his body? How many diapers did he change on a day when I did eight? If he, too, had changed eight, how many of his had been poopy? Who called the bank to see if we were overdrawn? Who loaded the dishwasher? Who washed the onesies? Who replaced the diaper table cover? Who remembered to buy the homeopathic colic pills? I watched it all like a hawk.

The less sleep I got, the more I counted. A friend of mine started referring to herself as "the sleep accountant" soon after her son was born. She took to asking friends, colleagues at work, and veritable strangers how much sleep they'd gotten the night before.

"What were you hoping," I'd asked, "that no one would have gotten less sleep than you, or that someone would be down in the bottom percentile keeping you company?"

"I was so jealous of people who were sleeping," she'd replied. "I just wanted to know who they were so I could hate them."

I, too, compared sleep with other people, especially

parents of young children, as well as time spent exercising and working nondomestically. All three counted, in my book, as vacation. But I wasn't driven to chart on paper anyone else's domestic labor—and freedom from it— against my own except Duncan's. He was my partner, damnit, and our children were a *joint project*. I'd never bought the argument (nor had he) that he was working as a professor "for us" while my complementary part of the deal was to hold down the homefront. In our house, work was what you did for yourself while housework and childcare were what you did for the family. We were both ambitious about our work, and we felt extremely fortunate to have work that we loved.

It was somewhat of an enigma to me how my work life had shrunk to so little and so much less than Duncan's. I was definitely the same ambitious person I'd always been. Three and a half hours of work, five days a week (and that was tops, and dependent on neither child being sick), was hardly enough. Why wasn't I doing more? In part, it was because I felt guilty since what I wanted to do—write poetry—seemed self-indulgent and impractical, absurdly so for a mother of young children.

Why couldn't I want to do something more lucrative or alternately, more maternal, like running a home daycare center? If I did something maternal, I could be with my children while also making money and being part of the working world. If I did something lucrative, Duncan's work would shrink in terms of the importance it held in our family—shrink down, possibly, to a level matching mine. If only I'd become an academic, I'd have a good chance of making the same salary Duncan did. If I'd kept working at nonprofits like NARAL, my salary wouldn't be far behind Duncan's. Why hadn't I done either of those things? The compulsion I felt to write, which had taken me away from my Ph.D. program and from nonprofit work as well, was fierce but also struck me as difficult to justify. How could someone's desire to write poetry stand up evenly against someone else's required departmental meeting or some tiny someone's need to eat from his major food source?

I was full of guilt and self-doubt, which made it hard to work, and full of frustration and desire to work more, which made it hard to mother. Often, the whole conundrum collapsed into anger at Duncan.

His work as a professor commanded more salary and respect in the world than my freelance and adjunct work did. And while his hours were indeed more flexible than those required by most jobs, they were still more rigid than mine. This meant it was often "reasonable" for me to be the one to handle whatever myriad business-hour errands, phone calls, and domestic tasks had to be done. Reason began to piss me off. Reason drove me to create Frequent Parenting Miles.

I wonder if my resentment would have been so extreme if Duncan had been supporting me financially, especially by working a job he hated just for money. But Duncan was doing exactly what he wanted to career-wise, and he wasn't bankrolling my writing or my time at home with the children. Instead, my grandmother had left me some money in her will the year before Joseph was born. It wasn't nearly enough to live on long-term, and more prudent folk would have certainly put it aside in a children's college fund, but I chose to use it earlier, buying myself time away from a traditional full-time job so I could write. I recognized my situation as extremely fortunate, and once again, felt guilty whenever I was unhappy. I also felt justified—sometimes—in resenting Duncan.

"Your job always trumps mine," I said a few nights after I'd begun my charting. We were in the kitchen cleaning up. Duncan was washing dishes, and I was dumping rice into Tupperware. "If some jerk calls a last-minute meeting in your department," I continued, "I take the kids, I do the shopping, whatever. You never take the kids while I'm working. You haven't done it once."

"I'd love to have four hours a day to write," Duncan said, wiping his brow with the back of his dish-soapy hand. "You think all of what I'm doing is fun? I race around all day, cutting corners everywhere I can, and I'm still not getting one-third of what I need to done. I'm exhausted. I can't do any more."

I started to tear up, hurt by his luxurious portrayal of my day. "I have four hours a day to be an adult! Three and a half if you subtract the time when I'm effectively a hooked-up cow. You're in the world of adults all day long. I know it's not all fun, but at least it's grown up. Except for three and a half hours, my whole life is domestic work and kid stuff. It's not fair, it's not fair at all."

"I took the kids last night so you could go to your book club," Duncan said.

"I hate my book club. We read really bad books, and it upsets me. For most of the women, book club is the only time they get away from their husband and kids, and that upsets me more. Something's got to change. I'm going crazy here."

"Let's write it down," Duncan said, "let's write everything down and see what's really going on."

"I plan to," I said, "I plan to write everything down."

✳✳✳

I kept domestic score for six months on my Frequent Parenting Miles chart because something—perhaps several somethings—seemed terribly askew, unfair, and traditional in our house, and I couldn't figure out what had caused it, how to prove its existence to Duncan, or how to stop it. The situation seemed to have sneaked up on Duncan and me, despite our mutual democratic intentions. It was as if some alien force, some ghost of marriages past, had slipped in one night when Joseph was an infant and we were sleeping, or more likely, taking turns trying to soothe his colicky cries. The ghost was tenacious, still present in our house forty months later. I went back to Joseph's infancy, again and again in my mind, trying to figure out how, why, and exactly when, we'd let the ghost in.

LIFE WITH BABY

When Joseph was born, Duncan and I were thrown into utter turmoil and extreme sleep deprivation, as many new parents are. We were also completely entranced by our son. In the first few weeks when we'd finally manage to get him down around 11 P.M. for the first two-hour chunk of night sleep, we'd go to the living room, rather than falling into bed ourselves, and watch the video we'd shot that afternoon of Joseph lying still, then every so often waving his tiny arms in the air. How miraculous! You could have knocked us over with a feather every time we saw it. Life was good, very good, and life was hard. "Did you wipe your ass today?" we joked to each other as we passed in the hall, rumpled, unshowered, clad in ratty T-shirts and sweats. If the answer was yes—and thank God, it always was—we could rest assured that we were still hanging on to the rudiments of civility.

Because of the way the semesters fell, Duncan had only eight more days of teaching after Joseph's birth—a period that my sister Celia spent with us helping out—then he had a six-week break from teaching. We did everything together during Duncan's break—marveled at the beauty of our son, worried about his every cry, ate dinner standing over the dryer where colicky Joseph lay and was soothed, consoled each other when we were too exhausted to move. We knew next to nothing about babies at the outset, and we learned side by side and together. It was after Duncan's break when our domestic situation began to shift, and to strike me as unfair, lonely, and remarkably traditional.

When Duncan was home and not grading or preparing for class, we continued to share everything except breast-feeding. Duncan did laundry, shopping, dishes, cleaning, changing diapers, strolling, bathing, and burping just like I did. He took to doing nearly all the cooking because Joseph always seemed to be nursing during the hour before dinner. I still did the lion's share of household organizational work as I had done before Joseph was born: calling the plumber, paying the bills, making changes to our drivers' insurance, scheduling doctors' appointments.

But Duncan was certainly no slouch. He wouldn't have any more sat on the couch reading the paper when he got home from work than held up a bank.

Still, I was doing full-on babycare and housework every weekday at home without him, and I continued doing it by his side all evening and night. Perhaps I should have gone out for a breather when Duncan came home, but I wanted to spend time with my husband, and Joseph was much needier in the evenings. Duncan wasn't away from the house twelve hours a day as an industrialist, doctor, or lawyer might have been, but he had a ton of work to do that first year of his job—at least sixty hours a week. Whenever possible he tried to grade papers and care for Joseph at the same time, and Joseph took many a short nap in the Snugli on Duncan's lap. But since I wasn't working for pay then, and Duncan was quite pressed by his new job, I felt I should do as much of the childcare as I possibly could.

When we'd discussed Joseph's care while he was still in utero, it had seemed entirely practical that I take a semester off from the M.F.A. program I'd just begun. Certainly this plan made much more sense, especially in terms of finances and breast-feeding, than Duncan taking time off from the job he would have just started three months before Joseph's birth. Never having had a baby, I didn't want to arrange hired childcare beforehand. Perhaps I'd morph into an earth mother and want to do everything myself. Whatever happened, I felt grateful and lucky to have the flexibility of a semester off. But by the end of January (Duncan had gone back to work on January 17), I was already wondering whether I could make it seven months as a stay-at-home mom. I definitely wasn't finding the job easy.

"How is it being home, enjoying a nice break from work?" my sixty-something neighbor asked one morning. The prior night had been hellacious, and I figured I'd gotten a total of four hours of sleep chopped into forty-five-minute-or-less increments. By 9 A.M., the time of our curbside chat, I'd been completely out of bed for three and a half hours, and I hadn't had time to eat, brush my hair, shower, or have a bowel movement yet.

"This is the hardest thing I've ever done," I said honestly, "and my last job, director of a pro-choice organization, involved death threats."

"Oh, oh, I see," she said, and it was clear that I'd horrified her. *Better not talk to that one again,* I imagined her telling herself as she hastily went back to pruning her roses.

Was I deliberately trying to be off-putting, even hostile? I wasn't sure. It had definitely irritated me that she'd used the phrase "nice break" in regard to infant care. Didn't she remember what it was like? Maybe her question had been innocent enough, though; maybe her own children had been calm and somnolent. But maybe not. Perhaps sleep deprivation causes paranoia, but at least once a day, I felt that something I read or someone I talked to—a stranger, acquaintance, old friend, midwife, my mother—made an assumption about how mothers are supposed to feel or act that wasn't at all true to my experience. And if the writer or interlocutor were a mother herself, I frequently found it hard to believe that the monolithic, lovely-lovely version of maternity I felt her putting forth could have possibly been 100 percent true to her own experience. Why were people lying to me, or at best telling sugar-coated half-truths?

Calm down, I would tell myself. *You might be reading too much into people's words.* On the other hand, I could just be observant, rooting out the maternal assumptions craftily slipped into seemingly innocuous phrases like "nice break," "total joy," "slowed-down pace," and "quality bonding time." If an assumption were posed as a question, shouldn't I answer honestly? Or was honesty itself—perhaps especially about motherhood—a hostile act?

Most days I was so tired that I did whatever took the least energy. Sometimes this was barking out the raw truth, sometimes it was telling a bland lie, other times I chose to smile weakly and say nothing at all.

By the time Duncan got home on a given day, I was more than ready for an ally, a partner who understood the challenges of infant care and didn't feel compelled to downplay them. Certainly Duncan knew how hard it was to care for infant Joseph. Except that he had never spent all day alone with Joseph. Even if Duncan had had the time (and he was extremely busy), breast-feeding prevented me from leaving Joseph for more than two and a half hours at a stretch.

My two-and-a-half-hour leash was not something either of us had anticipated or planned. When the midwives had warned us strongly about "nipple confusion," advising us not to introduce a bottle, under any circumstances, until six weeks for fear that Joseph would stop breast-feeding in favor of the easier-to-suck bottle, we'd heeded their admonition. All the baby books I'd read reiterated the midwives' advice as well. By six weeks, though, Joseph was decidedly inflexible on the matter, screaming bloody murder whenever he so much as caught a glimpse of a bottle out of the corner of his eye. Duncan, my mother, my sister, Duncan's mother, and Duncan's brother all tried tirelessly to get Joseph to take a bottle, but no luck.

Lesson number one, I told myself, was that breast-feeding, for all the good it may do (I'd read thirty-some articles and books on its benefits), impedes equitable parenting. The other major stumbling block to equity, as I saw it, was imbalanced careers.

When Duncan and I had met, we were on par—two graduate students working hard. In stark contrast, when Joseph was born three and a half years later, we had just relocated to faraway Austin because of Duncan's job—a perfect job for a historian in his field. And while I was technically a beginning M.F.A. student on leave, for all intents and purposes I worked as, felt like, and felt seen as an unemployed housewife and mother.

What the hell had happened, and whose fault was it? The decisions I'd recently made—to leave my Ph.D. program, to work at NARAL and then stop to pursue an M.F.A., to get pregnant, to move to Texas with Duncan—all seemed reasonable and positive on their own. Yet when taken in sum, these decisions also seemed to lead straight to an utterly traditional scenario: me at home alone with our baby while Duncan was at work.

Could this be my life? I'd spent the last fifteen years talking to anyone who would listen—especially boyfriends—about how to avoid this fate, and here I was living it! In Texas! Some days, the horror was too much to bear. In calmer moments, I told myself this was a temporary imbalance due to Joseph's infancy, Duncan's new job, and my current lesser earning capacity and greater flexibility as a student.

But what if the situation wasn't temporary? What if having a baby had slammed me into womanhood, with all the historic constrictions, in some irrevocable way? At 2 P.M. on a Tuesday, I *was* Jake Miller's mother except I didn't even make it out to volunteer at the hospital, to chat amicably with the other candy stripers and the nurses. Certainly, I had no time to knit. I did nothing except babycare and housework all day and most of the night, and I'd never worked so hard or been so tired in my life. I'd rarely been so angry.

My ex-boyfriend Alec was right; I had not grown up to be a maid. Yet wasn't a lot of what I was doing at home alone with a baby akin to what a maid would do? Come to think of it, I figured I was either working like a maid or a cow about 90 percent of the time. While Duncan thought, taught, and wrote (all of which I missed terribly), I cleaned, grocery-shopped, prepared meals, and breast-fed. My daily work came entirely from my body while Duncan's came primarily from his mind. In this way, we defined people of different classes. Duncan had held on in the middle class, and I'd been demoted.

It's unnerving, lonely, and infuriating to feel separated in such stark terms from someone you used to be like, someone you still call partner. While I had moved into a shockingly separate sphere, I knew full well that I hadn't dropped a class notch while Duncan stayed put. Nothing more

clearly marks a contemporary American woman as middle-
or upper-middle class, after all, than stay-at-home breast-
feeding motherhood. No one else can afford to do it.
As I stayed home with Joseph for seven months, I recognized the time as an economic luxury and berated
myself accordingly whenever I felt unhappy. I was just a
spoiled middle-class princess feeling sorry for myself
because I suddenly had to do a lot of metaphoric and lit-
eral shitwork. Look how privileged I was to be able to
spend precious time with my baby, time many mothers
didn't have! Shame on me for being miserable some of
the time instead of grateful. Shame, shame! I felt like I
had ten years earlier at Harvard: privileged and guilty, yet
simultaneously furious that I was less privileged than my
boyfriend, or, in this case, husband.

Here was Duncan, after all, with a beautiful son and
the dream job he'd always wanted. Come to think of it,
the only thing riding his ass—other than lack of sleep, a
dirty house, pressure to get tenure, and the stress of meeting new colleagues—was an angry wife. I wasn't proud of
myself, but I figured the harder I rode, the more he might
just grasp how I was feeling. Except that my feelings were
anything but uniform.

I was overcome with love for Joseph and grateful that
I didn't have to leave him. I felt that I loved him more
than I'd ever loved anyone, which unnerved and surprised me at times: Was there something wrong because I
seemed to love Duncan, my sister, my brother, and everyone else less? How could I love someone so much who
couldn't talk?

It was clear to me, even in my emotionally high state,

though, that loving Joseph didn't mean I didn't also want to pursue work of my own. Why should it? This was the maternal assumption I found hardest to take, whatever the source—the Johnson & Johnson television ad of a shining blond mother in perfectly pressed stay-at-home khakis bathing a child while Dad-with-briefcase smiled from the doorway, our midwives' recommendation to breast-feed "on demand" until age two or even three, or a bank teller's comment when I came to make a deposit with Joseph in tow that it must be "just about nap time, time to catch up on that laundry!" The cultural cues I saw all around made me feel it was wrong to want what should have been reasonable enough: meaningful work in the world *and* love.

I thought a lot about work and love in the interspersed quiet moments when I was home alone with Joseph. The separate spheres I'd witnessed and rejected so strongly at Jake Miller's house, and was now living a version of myself, seemed dependent on men primarily choosing work and women primarily choosing love, and the work that goes with sustaining that love. To pass the time at home, I took to asking myself a series of wrenching theoretical questions on the subject. Here was one: If someone held a gun to my head and said, "Choose love or work, choose the life of a traditional middle-class woman or that of a traditional middle-class man," what would I do?

Woman, I realized. I'd choose the traditional woman's life, hands down. This would never have been my answer pre-Joseph. Now, I told myself, I'd choose the woman's path even if there were no possibility of hired childcare, stealing from my own sleep to work from 3 A.M. to 5 A.M.

(the best bet for no interruptions in our current house-hold), then again in the afternoon as I played a barrage of gentle kid videos the moment Joseph was old enough to have an interest. I'd squeeze time out for work whenever I could, fortunate that at least part of what I wanted to do work-wise could be done at home, and hope that I could get enough time—and stay awake in that time—so that I wouldn't go mad.

"I had to take Prozac to do it, but I stayed at home with my children," a woman told *Talk Magazine* right before the publication folded. What self-awareness! She knew her particular depression was circumstantial, and she got some drugs to alleviate it. Given how I was faring so far as a stay-at-home mother, I felt I was definitely looking at a Prozac prescription if I took the role on long-term, or possibly even heavier drugs. Thank God the drugs were out there.

I'd go through whatever it took, I told myself—if forced at gunpoint—because once I had Joseph, it was clear to me that long-houred work away from him would have been more wrenching to me than any of the adjust-ments I'd have to make to function as a stay-at-home mother. Yes, provided I had the money, I'd pick love over work just like generations of middle-class women before me had done, some feeling it primarily as a privilege, oth-ers primarily as an oppression. And as I made this choice, I'd remind Duncan—subtly but daily—of the sacrifice it entailed and the morally superior position it afforded me. What other power would I have to hold up against his economic and professional power?

But there was no gun. A new millennium was on the

horizon as I stayed home with Joseph in 1995, contemplating these either-or theoreticals. I didn't have to choose work or love. I was fortunate enough to be of a generation and an economic class who could have both. I wanted Duncan to have both. I wanted to be with him because he wanted both, just like I did. We both believed 100 percent in the joint project. We just weren't living it.

RUNNING AWAY

There were periods of greater and lesser equity between Duncan and me during the next four years. I went back to graduate school when Joseph was seven months old and while I attended the ten-day residencies that my program required, I continued to breast-feed and parent, but Duncan did the lion's share of the childcare then. Summer weeks when Duncan wasn't teaching or doing research were much nearer to equitable than weeks during the school season. The months when we didn't have a breast-feeding infant were also less imbalanced.

I started keeping track of our Frequent Parenting Miles at a time of extreme frustration for me. Joseph was three-and-a-half, and I'd been waiting since his birth for Duncan and me to hit a 50/50 division of childcare and housework. To my mind, we still hadn't done it. Now Duncan was particularly pressed at work because he had to finish his book manuscript in time for tenure review. Once again, reason suggested a plan that was difficult for me to fully embrace. Surely I should do even more at home with our baby and three-year-old so he could complete his book. I could see the logic, but it didn't stop my resentment. I created Frequent Parenting Miles, in part, to help me hang on and do what was necessary through a period of clear inequity—the last one, as far as I was concerned. With Frequent Parenting Miles, I'd have a record of all the domestic work I'd done so when Duncan finished his book, we could reverse roles, or at least enter a true 50/50 split.

The fact that I, too, was writing a book (of poems) fed my resentment. With children as young as ours, it didn't seem possible that we both go full-steam ahead on such time-consuming projects. I could see that it was utterly reasonable for Duncan to go first since he was further along in his work and he had an externally defined deadline, but I was still angry. It made me more angry to note that the pattern we were living was reflected all around us by other couples. Did these couples also have a plan to role-reverse after some specific event, like the receipt of tenure? Maybe they did, and the event had already passed, and nothing had changed. Would this happen to Duncan and me?

The way we were living—me doing the majority of the childcare and housework and a little work of my own while Duncan concentrated more fully on his career— was completely normalized in our circle of friends, and it definitely didn't end once a baby stopped nursing. I was actually much better off than most married women I knew. Friends and neighbors would often compliment Duncan's fathering while complaining bitterly about their own husbands' lesser efforts. I was angry, but I could see that Duncan was doing way more household work than any father of young kids I knew, with the exception of one. But other men weren't my standard. My standard was *me*. As long as Duncan was doing less than I was, I was angry.

Something had to change. Duncan may have been under extreme pressure at work, but I had to know that our situation was temporary. Frequent Parenting Miles was my insurance policy. Without the visibility it offered, I was afraid something might just have to break.

The wives of two men in Duncan's department had left their husbands, abruptly, right after the men got tenure. Both women, it turned out, had been having affairs during the months when their husbands were working around the clock. A third historian's wife, Colleen, had accosted Duncan or me every time she saw us to rail against her husband while he was preparing for tenure—a time that coincided, as it later did for Duncan and me—with the infancy of a child.

"I'm doing *everything* right now," she told us one evening as we walked by with baby Joseph in his stroller. She'd practically bowled us over as she raced out on the sidewalk to catch us and share her angry tale. "I'm doing every single thing in this house—with a newborn, and two preschoolers at home! It's killing me, but I'm not going to let Richard ever say 'I didn't get tenure because you made me clean the toilet.' "

It was my distinct impression that many wives associated with UT's history department were fed up, even if most of us tried to hide it from one another. We hid it because the imbalances we were living were embarrassing; most of us had advanced degrees, and many of us were feminists. How had we ended up in such traditional positions within our marriages? If love was the culprit, then love sucked, I decided, and I set my sights on work.

I applied for a two-week writing fellowship, which if I won, I planned to take three months after Duncan was certain he'd be finished with his manuscript. The fellowship would be my Frequent Parenting Trip, and when I got back, I promised myself I'd try to wipe the slate clean, even put the slate away, provided we were finally able to move on to a true 50/50 split.

When I got notice that I'd won the fellowship, I was ecstatic, guilty, and terrified. How could I leave my young children for two weeks? Ben was eighteen months old and Joseph was just four. And Duncan was still not finished with his book. I postponed my fellowship another three months, which I didn't entirely mind since the delay moved Ben that much further from babyhood.

"I'm going this time," I told Duncan. "I can't push it back any more."

"Okay," he said. "I'll be ready."

When he wasn't, he decided to take the children to his parents' house so they could help with the childcare while he continued to edit his manuscript. I felt guilty about the setup and worried about the disruption to my in-laws, but I was firmly committed to going. Duncan assured me he could handle everything, and he wanted me to go. "You deserve it," he said. "It's your turn."

✳✳✳

The fellowship took place at an artist's retreat on the grounds of a Franciscan monastery. Two painters and two other writers—all women—and I shared a house.

There was also a resident manager, who wrote poetry, living on-site.

"I took the liberty of reading your application package," he told me the first night. "I have a key to everything so I just got your poetry out of the director's drawer. It's awesome—you're an amazing writer."

"Thanks," I said.

"I don't want to bother you or anything, but would you take a look at some of my work? I'd love to have your perspective."

"I'm not sure when I can get to it, but okay," I said with clear reluctance in my voice. *I just want to be left alone,* I was thinking. *I've come here to get away from men, boys, and their needs. Is no place in the world safe or private?*

Tom was respectful of my working time over the next few days, though he did slip his poems under my closed door nearly every day. I didn't have to see his words, though, because he'd folded the pages shut, sealing the edge with odd orange stickers.

One afternoon when I was completely stuck on a section I was writing, I looked at his poems. They were bad, I thought, but there was one about me. Jesus, he liked my hair—he thought it looked like Anne Sexton's. It didn't, but I was flattered, and angry. He was flirting with me, inserting himself and his desire into my desperately needed time away. And despite the reference to Anne Sexton's hair, he'd constructed me primarily as a muse in his poem. A muse? *I could write circles around you,* I thought. *Don't you dare make me static and feminine. Maybe I should take* you *as a muse.*

I was talking to Duncan and the children every night. I

was loving the long days of work and also missing my family terribly. The night after I looked at Tom's poems, I told Duncan that Tom was bugging me, asking for feedback on his shitty poems just when I had this incredibly rare time away from students who needed my commentary and children who needed juice or a diaper change. Although I didn't say it, I was also at the writer's retreat to be away from Duncan and the way I couldn't stop myself from counting everything I thought he wasn't doing.

"Tell him you can't," Duncan said about Tom's demand for editorial comment, "or better yet, just rip the poems up. You don't have time for this." He paused a second, then added, "Does he have a crush on you?"

"I think so," I said sheepishly.

"I knew it!" Duncan said. "I could tell he wanted to get into your pants as soon as I saw him. The sneaky jerk." Duncan had met Tom briefly the previous weekend when he and the kids had dropped me off.

"No one's getting in my pants," I said. "I'm working. Besides, Tom is bald and chubby."

"What are you saying? What if he were incredibly good-looking?"

"He's not," I said.

"Thank God," Duncan replied.

"Yeah, thank God," I agreed.

✳✳✳

Tom was physically less than gorgeous (so was I, of course), but he was oddly compelling—at least to me, then. Over the course of the meals we shared, I learned that he'd been a coke addict, his parents were entirely dysfunctional in ways that interested me, and he was a passionate Catholic. He seemed to still have a fairly serious drinking problem.

"Come to Mass with me," he said one morning.

"I can't, I'm allergic to wheat," I replied, which he found to be hilarious.

I liked when people thought I was funny. Duncan and I had recently had a huge argument about this very issue.

"Other people laugh at what I say! You never laugh," I'd accused Duncan. "Why don't you laugh? I'm dark, but sometimes I'm funny, too. When you don't laugh, it makes me feel like you don't really see me, or that you wish my edges would just go away."

"Please, let's not go there again," Duncan said with exhaustion. "I don't want you to be the girl next door, okay? I don't want you to be nice and boring. I'll try harder, I swear I will. I'll try hard to laugh at your jokes."

"People can't *try* to laugh. What are you saying? Either you find me funny or you don't. Which is it?"

"I find you funny—I do. I don't know why I'm not laughing."

Duncan and I had often noted how different we were, how different our pasts had been. He hadn't taken drugs or had as many sex partners or been deliberately engaged with angst the way I had. Instead, he'd spent a transformative year on a remote farm and sung in a series of professional choirs. We were a marital Mutt and Jeff: Mr. Wholesome and Ms. Dazed and Confused.

Tom's past was considerably edgier than mine. He'd been a roadie for a punk band, a bartender in a brothel; and his ex-wife had slit her wrists one night while he was in the bathroom. I realized during my days at the retreat that I missed hanging out with people like Tom. My druggie friends had, for the most part, grown up, as I had. They certainly weren't living in Austin. Many other druggies were, of course—arguably more per capita than anywhere else in the U.S. But I didn't want to hang out with twenty-somethings who were still floundering. I wanted to hang out with older, wiser ex–drug experimenters who valued what they'd done and where they'd been even as they saw fit to change their ways. With the exception of his still-excessive drinking, Tom was like this. He was funny, ironic, self-perceptive, and full of energy. He talked much better than he wrote, and we took to talking in the evenings—sometimes with the other residents, sometimes just the two of us.

There was definite sexual tension between us, which frightened and thrilled me. I'd come away to work, and I was working—harder than I had in years—but I also began to flirt. Was I crazy? I was a married woman! And my timing seemed particularly ironic and unfair.

While Duncan and I were definitely having problems—almost all related to our division of domestic labor and how his lack of doing what I perceived to be enough felt like a lack of support for me and my work—he and his parents were certainly supporting me strongly right then. *Great timing,* I told myself. Here you are, having intimate, late-night conversations with a compelling, if physically less-than-perfect, man while your husband and in-laws take care of your children. Way to go in leading the crowd in selfishness!

But why couldn't I have a tiny taste of selfishness? Where was the harm? Didn't I deserve a little flattery after working my ass—and breasts—off for four years, taking up all the slack as Duncan finished his book, living in a place I was growing increasingly disenchanted with just because Duncan had a job there?

Talking late at night to an ex–coke addict hardly seemed to even the score. Still, it was dangerous, and I knew it. I liked the danger, the attention, and the praise Tom continued to give me. I also liked that I was the one with more power. I was the writer on fellowship, and Tom was the less-accomplished apprentice.

In my marriage, I was the apprentice, and Duncan was the professional. I'd abandoned academia fairly late in the game, then worked at NARAL, and only when I was thirty had I started seriously learning to write. In the meantime, Duncan had continued to move forward on his original path, passing me in terms of power, salary, and sheer amount of pages produced. There was nothing justifiable in my anger about this, or my envy—I'd made my own choices, after all, as Duncan was fond of reminding me. Still, I felt both anger and envy whenever I thought about how much more power in the world Duncan had than I did. I hated our imbalanced careers almost as much as I hated our imbalanced domestic labor. And I saw the two as utterly linked, which often sent me on a whole new cycle of anger—sometimes self-directed, often pointed at Duncan.

I realized while on retreat that I was absolutely furious at Duncan. I'd suspected this, but now I had total clarity. My flirtation with Tom was unquestionably fueled by my anger. It was difficult to feel sexual toward someone I was furious at. How much easier to turn my gaze toward someone else I didn't have to negotiate childcare or housework with.

"If I'd been with you in that house for two weeks, I bet you'd have fallen in love with me again," Duncan said during the first huge argument we had upon my return. It was true, and it made me deeply sad.

Duncan and I lived like worker bees, passing in the day, sometimes without even stopping before we barked out the questions and terse answers that too often passed for conversation. "Did you remember to pick up the blah-blah from blah-blah? To call the whosit about whatsit?" I'd ask as soon as I saw him, and Duncan would respond with a yes or a guilty no.

At night, Duncan often worked late, determined not to put more stress on me by doing all his work during the kids' waking hours. I couldn't remember the last time we'd had an intimate conversation, just for the joy of talking, rather than as some kind of argument.

We had a very rough year after I returned from the retreat, our roughest yet. We went to couples therapy, and we fought a lot. Duncan felt that our marriage had reached a crisis point, and that everything began to fall apart when I took up—however incompletely—with Tom. I felt, on the other hand, that Duncan and I had finally turned a corner, that he truly saw the severity of my anger. I was ashamed that it took the threat of another man to make Duncan see how furious and demoralized I was. What an age-old feminine wile. How embarrassing that I'd sunk so low.

Why hadn't my meticulous Frequent Parenting Miles chart worked, or any of the countless explanations I'd made about power, housework, love, work, and the creative process—many of which Duncan agreed with in theory? I didn't know, but that was now the past. While I hadn't consciously flirted with Tom—and told Duncan about it—in order to get Duncan's attention, I now had his attention, as well as his anger. I intended to focus the attention part, as best I could, on making what I viewed as critical changes in our division of domestic labor.

I'm not suggesting that flirting with other men is a good way to get a husband to do more housework and childcare. I can't imagine this working across the board. And it's a simplification of what happened in our case. My flirtation was the catalyst that got us into therapy, though, and ultimately began the process of us listening better to each other and building a marriage that is stronger and more equitable now. I'm sorry that I resorted to something so drastic, adolescent, and retrograde, but I also can't help noting that it worked.

HOME AGAIN

Duncan and I began to live what I would call the joint project ten months after I came back from the retreat. Duncan got tenure, which was followed by a semester off. While he was frustrated about not getting much work done during his time off, he was also willing to take the children on alternate afternoons so I could work longer hours than I ever had. "You need this semester off more than I do," he said.

Since that spring of 2000, we've pretty much spent the same amount of time on work, and almost the same on housework and childcare. I'm not charting anymore, but I believe I still put in slightly more hours at home. I definitely get more accomplished in my hours because I can multitask better. What a horrid skill to possess.

Part of what took us so long to reach this point of near-equity was the degree to which I did believe in the Cinderella myth. I wanted, or half-wanted, to be transformed by love, made less petty and more generous. I still want this, in fact. Instead, I often found myself confronted—particularly as I faced Duncan—with my old self: furious at the slightest injustice, desirous of power, quick to judge, and quicker still to count. Part of me was distinctly glad that my old self hadn't gone away: Who would I be if I suddenly embraced maternal sacrifice and the domestic arts with no eye to what my partner was doing in the meantime? I had to hold on to my edges and my evaluative eye in order to remember who I was. And Duncan had to realize what was at stake if we didn't share the domestic work equitably, which was nearly everything.

Every six months or so, a new book comes out enumerating men's and women's respective work at home. If I'm a bean counter, these authors make a profession of it. I eat these titles up, calling the most egregious facts out to Duncan with glee: "Only five percent of married American men ever do a stitch of laundry! Thirteen percent of men under forty-five sit around—just sit on their butts—while their wives make dinner! Women work sixty percent harder than men in the hour between seven and eight A.M. and seventy-two percent harder between six and seven P.M. If you give a man in Brazil money, he spends seventy percent on cigars and liquor. If you give the money to a woman, she will spend ninety percent on her children."*

"No way!" Duncan will say, or "Stop telling me crazy lies!"

We'll move to sit together on the sofa, incredulous about the things most men don't do, and firmly on the same side. It's a delicate alliance, though, and we have firsthand knowledge of how bad things can get—at least for us—when the alliance isn't fully there. We also know it's something we'll have to shore up over and over again.

---

* See especially Ann Crittenden, *The Price of Motherhood* (New York: Metropolitan Books, 2001) and Susan Maushart, *WifeWork* (New York: Bloomsbury, 2002).

FIVE

Judging Friends

Once again, my story begins at Jake Miller's house. In August of 1980, my friend Christine and I were spending the weekend at Jake's, along with Jake's friend, Richard, who was Christine's boyfriend. We were all upcoming seniors in high school. Richard and Christine were already having full-fleshed sex; Jake and I were not. But we'd been getting encouragement—privately, girl to girl and boy to boy—from Richard and Christine. The four of us had agreed that Jake and I would attempt the shift that very weekend.

At 3 A.M., I got up from the pullout double bed I was sharing with Christine in Mr. Miller's home office and started creeping upstairs. I met Richard on the landing. He had just dislodged from the camping mat he'd been lying on beside Jake's twin bed.

"Break a leg," Richard whispered. Jesus, I didn't want to think about things breaking! I kept walking.

I got to Jake's room, and we de-virginicized ourselves in his childhood bed. It was a bit awkward, certainly strange, and it hurt—though thankfully not anywhere near how I imagined the split of a leg bone. There was a tiny spot of blood, and that was it. I'd been transformed.

"How do you feel?" Jake asked.

"Different."

"Yeah, me too."

We lay there for a while, holding each other, contemplating the change. I wasn't happy, per se, or particularly sad, though I do recall a distinct sense of disappointment. Was this it—what everyone went on and on about, the act capable of causing major tragic events like the Trojan War? Clearly, there was something I wasn't yet grasping.

I didn't want to relay my disappointment to Jake—we'd both been through enough trauma for one night—plus it was already four-thirty, our prearranged time of switchback. Mr. Miller got up early to play golf, and we couldn't risk being caught in the wrong beds when he dragged his clubs out of the hall closet.

"I love you," I told Jake. He responded in kind, and I tiptoed downstairs.

I found Richard wrapped around Christine, both of them asleep. "It's time to get up," I whispered, nudging Christine's leg.

Richard jumped to his feet, too-big boxers precariously gripping his waist, and Chris beckoned for me to crawl in beside her. "How was it?" she asked excitedly. "Did you do it?"

"Yeah, I did," I said with a smile. I slipped into the body-warmed sheets, and Chris squeezed my hand. We talked intensely for hours. I told her second by second about the sex, how it seemed so much less than what I'd expected, how it hurt, how I wondered in what ways it would change my relationship with Jake. I worried that things would somehow be worse. She reciprocated with a retelling of her own first intercourse, which I had initially heard blow by blow four hours after its occurrence, but was delighted to revisit since I had even more questions now. What did having sex mean? How could we feel relieved to be rid of our virginity and also sad that it was gone? Why was virginity so much more precious in girls than in boys? What would happen now?

One thing, at least, was utterly clear: The loss of my virginity would have been much lonelier, sadder, and more confusing if Chris hadn't been just downstairs to welcome me into her bed for a long postmortem.

Jake and I were close, and we did talk about sex, our relationship, our parents, our future, and our friends, but in many ways, Chris and I were closer. Certainly, she and I had spent more nights together. We'd shared countless sleepovers since meeting at the beginning of tenth grade, and we slept easily beside each other, familiar with the other's nighttime breathing. We knew each other's bodies nearly as well as we knew our own. We scrutinized them together. *My thighs are too fat. No, they're not. Do you think I need to bleach my lip? I don't think you have to.*

The night I lost my virginity then climbed into bed with Chris epitomizes my understanding of female friendship in my teens and twenties: a place of deep physical and emotional intimacy, as well as sense-making talk. At times it seemed like my whole life consisted of doing bizarre and occasionally painful things with boys, then dissecting those actions in intimate conversations with girls immediately afterward.

I was aware that this was a flawed model for living. For one thing, I knew that most people, both male and female, would view my talks with girls as less significant than the actions we talked about. Certainly on the night of August 10, 1980, the big event, the subject of the question "Did you do it?" was intercourse with Jake, not discourse with Christine. Likewise, when people ask "What happened?" in reference to a football game, they mean *on the field, between the football players*, not in regard to whatever words the sideline cheerleaders might have shouted.

The hierarchy of action with boys above talk with girls made me sad and angry. It also didn't hold true to my experience. For me, talk was the connective tissue of my life, the place where I made sense of the world. I wasn't a brooder or a loner as a teen; I was a talker. And there were endless things that needed discussion. Without the daily talks I had with Chris, Vicky, Amanda, and Renata, my life might be nothing more than a series of disjointed, confusing, and painful events. Was this in fact what it was? Not as long as I had girlfriends.

Because I was aware of the world's ranking of action over talk, I deliberately tried to do more things with girls, as well as attempting more intimate conversation with boys, but the split remained somewhat intact. I would go to the beach with a girlfriend, but what stuck with me was not the swimming; it was what we talked about as we lay on our towels, staring out at the waves. I valued talk so highly that it didn't feel like I was giving myself and other girls short shrift when we didn't go anywhere at all, instead just sitting and talking in our bedrooms. While the choices weren't always this stark, I would so much rather get ready for a junior high dance with my mother and sister or do a dissection of the couples at the dance afterward with my childhood friend Vicky than actually be there with my hair up in an uncomfortable bun, dancing awkwardly with someone in a pale blue tuxedo I didn't particularly like. Of course the dance, the heterosexual moment under the glittery STAIRWAY TO HEAVEN banner, was the fodder for our pre- and post-conversations. I didn't like this dependence on the dance, but I had to admit that I found the material endlessly interesting.

If a junior prom could provoke hours of scintillating discussion, and the loss of my virginity could lead to months and months of talk with a handful of close female friends, surely becoming a mother would be a conversational bonanza. I had grown someone else inside my body, and now he was out in the world! What might he do? What should I do in response?

The sheer rudiments of the situation defined freaky and amazing. The freaky, the amazing, and the human have always been my favorite elements for conversation. I couldn't wait to sit down and talk it all out with Chris, with Vicky, with Renata, with Alice, with Melinda, and with Celia. Except that I was incredibly busy as a new mother and very, very tired. I managed to call all of my significant friends once—to tell them that Joseph had arrived and to briefly explore the meaning of this change—and then I didn't speak to many of them again for six months.

As a recent transplant to Texas, all of my old friends lived at least 1,500 miles away. Furthermore, with the exception of Alice, my college roommate who lived in Berlin and was exceedingly hard to get on the phone due to time zone issues coupled with the demands of our two young babies, none of my friends had children yet. I was incredibly eager to make new friends in town, especially friends who were new mothers. If childbirth is a helluva time to give up drugs, new motherhood is a helluva time to give up friends. Never had I needed intimate, sense-making talk with women more.

I wasn't sure where best to look for new mother friends. In the past, I'd always had a social context for making friends: school or job. Now, as a woman at home with an infant in a town where I knew no one, I needed a plan. Should I simply prowl the suburban streets around our rental house, pouncing on any woman with a stroller? Would I inherently have an immediate kinship with any woman who had a baby, or did I need to be more selective? If so, how?

I was too new at motherhood to fully know what kind of a mother I was, other than tired. Perhaps I would be an earth mother–type, mashing my own baby puree with a mortar and pestle. On the other hand, I might need a friend who wouldn't disapprove if I employed every appliance and shortcut in the book. Would I favor a strict or laissez-faire approach to bedtime and feedings? Would we cosleep or use a crib? I didn't rightly know, but I felt that these decisions would have some relevance on my friend-making. Meagan Dodson, in her essay "Parental Judgment," says she created an elaborate "friend-o-meter" as a new mother, a yardstick against which to assess potential friends: "Does she breast-feed? Ten points. Past a year? Twenty. Well, she works part-time, but only while her husband is home with the kids, so we'll only knock off five points for that."*

I didn't have any criteria nearly this concrete yet, but I feared other mothers might, and that I'd be found lacking in some critical arena. It made sense to me that mothers would want to be friends with other women whom they viewed as good mothers. After all, shouldn't the qualities of a good mother and a good friend be the same: compassion, empathy, a willingness to listen, and joie de vivre? I wanted to figure out how to be a good mother primarily for Joseph's sake and my own, but I also figured this transformation would have the added benefit of making me an attractive friend for other mothers. I'd work on becoming a good mother, and at the same time, I'd look for situations in which to make mother-friends.

One day as I was rather forlornly strolling infant Joseph to the grocery store, I saw a baby gymnastics class advertised on a telephone pole. The flyer said that physical stimulation to a baby's body—garnered from rolling backward on large rubber balls—would integrate his brain synapses. An additional plus, the flyer went on, was meeting other concerned parents "like you." I wanted Joseph's brain to be integrated—certainly I did—and I was eager to meet other new parents. How wonderful to accomplish both with one little class! On the appointed first day, I strapped four-month-old Joseph into his car seat and drove over to the abandoned elementary school gym where the class was being held.

---

* Meagan Dodson, "Parental Judgment," *Brain, Child*, Summer 2002: 20.

Joseph did not like his first Gymboree class—if shrieking nonstop was any indication of his mood. He kept blinking at the bright lights in the huge gymnasium and recoiling from the shocking red, blue, and yellows of the tumbling equipment. Nor did he like the class finale: us moms holding an enormous parachute over our babies who squirmed below on red tumble mats while Miss Kimmy, our instructor, blew bubbles above the children's faces, and we all sang "The Farmer in the Dell" as loudly and enthusiastically as we could. I had to drop my edge of the parachute in order to bend down and pick up an utterly distressed Joseph. Miss Kimmy looked askance. The parachute was meant to be an "independent moment." Too bad, Miss Kimmy. My child needed me, and moreover, I needed the comfort of his sweet body pressed against mine as well right then. If I'd been any less self-conscious, I might have been shrieking along with my son.

What, exactly, did I find wrong with this scenario? Call me overly intellectual or lacking in a sense of play, but I realized I didn't want to sing "The Farmer in the Dell" with a group of other white women on a Tuesday at 10 A.M. I might be cajoled to do this—ideally in a more heterogeneous group—on a Saturday, but Tuesday morning was still sacred in my mind. Tuesday was for work. Truth be told, I started to fantasize about work as I stood there singing about the dell. *Quick,* I thought, *let me call the other Dell, the high-powered Austin one, and beg them to hire me even though I'm barely computer literate. If they won't hire me, maybe they can just rent me a small cubicle so I can sit there and pretend to be part of the adult world that matters again.*

I felt split—deeply so. I didn't want to miss a second of Joseph's day—I could get weepy sometimes if Duncan gave him a bath without me—but after four months of full-on mom duty, I was also getting antsy to rejoin the larger adult world. Throughout my days at home as a full-time mother, I missed the world of working adults periodically, but the hunger was near constant at Gymboree.

I knew as I witnessed and participated in the scene of exhausted mothers dutifully pushing their babies through padded tunnels that I should be thinking something open-minded like, *Well, whatever a woman wants to do. Thank goodness we have more choices now. Those who want to and can afford to stay home should for as long as they choose or can, and those who want to or have to work, should, without any guilt.* But I didn't feel anything nearly as laissez-faire as this. *What a waste of womanpower!* I thought. *Why are we here? Do our children really need this? Do we need it? There must be a better plan than one woman alone all day with one baby, except for a brief and fairly unpleasant forty-five minute Gymboree class.*

Immediately I berated myself: *Stop it, stop judging! You have no idea what's best for these probably very diverse women. What's wrong with you that you can't sing delightful children's songs in a cheerful way? You're too cerebral. Learn something new! Go with the flow.*

But the flow depressed me and struck me as indicative of a larger structural wrong, a wrong I didn't want to participate in. True, I had no idea what was going on in most of the other households in Austin, or America for that matter, and this was only one small—if nationally syndicated—baby gymnastics class. But if I were here, didn't it mean I thought it was okay that the only visible people out with children on a Tuesday at 10 A.M. were white middle-class women? I did not think this was okay, not in the least. I found it wrong that other women couldn't have more time with their children, that fathers couldn't—or didn't—take more time with their children, and that stay-at-home women couldn't also do something that would make their minds and spirits feel alive in ways I distinctly did not see in evidence under the parachute. I couldn't bear the thought that this class would be a grown woman's only social contact on a given day. More personally, I didn't see how I would make it if it became mine.

I loved being with Joseph. I would kiss his sweet baby head, his chubby pink fingers, his toes, at least ten times a minute. Loving a baby is a very visceral experience. It was physically painful to be away from his tiny body and self, and I was grateful, on a daily basis, that I didn't yet have to be. Was it love for Joseph, though, that had brought me to Gymboree? It was a factor. What I didn't like—and this distaste grew stronger and stronger as I went to more mom-and-baby activities—was the way these events struck me as public displays of that love. *Look at me, look at me! See, I'm someone who loves my baby, I'm available all day to roll her on a ball or whatever else she needs. I'm a good mother, really, I am.*

I had no credentials as a mind reader, but I felt certain that this unspoken conversation was going on around me, and I really didn't want to join in. I didn't want to evaluate other mothers, and I definitely didn't want them to evaluate me. Someone with a ticking friend-o-meter was probably looking at me right then, seeing how I measured up. I needed friends desperately, but did I have to pass a test to get them? What, exactly, were the questions on the exam?

The biggie, as I imagined it, was, Are you a selfless mother, or a selfish one? And the first indicator of the answer was whether you were at home (or Gymboree) with your baby, or at work.

I knew this was a retrograde yardstick, and more important, that only a tiny minority of the world's women had the financial luxury to even seriously consider it. The fact that I was in this minority made me guilty. I was also angry. What a cruel choice for any woman, especially one who loved her work, to have to make.

While I truly missed the two kinds of work I'd been doing prior to Joseph's birth—social activism and solitary writing—I missed work, in general (even a fantasy Dell job I was utterly unqualified for), more acutely at Gymboree because I knew work was where the dads were. If any men had been under the parachute, I might not have felt so angry about being there. I might have been better able to focus on what was truly enjoyable: watching Joseph chuckle as I bounced him up and down on a hippity-hop, the smell of the big blue ball and how it reminded me of my own childhood hopping down the street with my sister, the way the sun streamed through the ceiling windows, striking the mats in accordionlike rays. But I was too angry— and simultaneously too guilty—to sustain this kind of enjoyment for more than a moment.

What Gymboree needed was a revolution! What could I do? Force Duncan to skip work so he could come every week in the name of equity? Surreptitiously get the addresses of the other mom-baby duos, go to their houses in the evening, and kick their husbands in the ass? Collect money from the current moms for a scholarship fund, then persuade the bosses of working-class mothers to let them out for an hour to come to Gymboree? Surely they'd want to do something better than Gymboree if they got that time off.

In graduate school, when I'd been involved in organizing a union, the adversary was clear as a bell: the Yale administration. Who was there even to organize against this time? Miss Kimmy? She was just trying to make a living. I sensed an evil at Gymboree, but I couldn't quite pinpoint the culprit.

Over the next few years, it became clear in our particular household that while Duncan would occasionally attend Mom-and-me events like Gymboree, he never would have gone through the steps of signing up our children for any of these classes. If they were going to tremble terrified under a multicolored parachute, bang sticks together and sing about a British pony, or play the violin while still in diapers, it would be on my initiative. Perhaps I, myself, was the enemy, or at least the one to blame for my unhappiness under the parachute. Buying into this crazy propaganda about brain synapses, thinking Gymboree would be useful and fun for Joseph and for me—what an idiot! I deserved all the middle-class mother malaise I was feeling, and I'd best take action to snap out of it.

I asked Duncan to go to Gymboree the following week. I wanted his opinion—was all of this back-rolling really good for Joseph?—and I wanted him to go for equity's sake. I was the only one who could breast-feed our son, but I wasn't the only one who could roll him on a big red ball. I also wanted Duncan's take on the other moms. Shouldn't I be able to find at least one friend here? The women all looked reasonable and nice. Friendship is a mysterious process, but I'd always managed to find at least one or two intimate friends without a whole lot of difficulty in every town I'd lived in before. Our group was racially and socioeconomically homogenous, and Gymboree's activities were loud and irritating, but couldn't I still possibly strike up an engaging conversation with somebody in the lobby after class? I'd already paid our tuition, and I didn't, truthfully, know of any better place to meet new mothers.

Over spring break, Duncan took Joseph to Gymboree. It was a particularly hectic morning following a more-sleepless-than-usual night, so Duncan was neither shaved nor showered when he arrived at class. (Often, I was in an equal state of dishevelment when I got there.) I relished the hour and fifteen minutes Joseph and Duncan were gone, though it was hardly enough time to reclaim myself as a productive, empowered adult. I took a shower and stared dumbly at a book of essays on poetry. A *still comes before B*—that was about all I could muster, thought-wise.

When Duncan got back, I asked how it had gone. "The moms didn't like me," he said. "They glared when I sang harmony."

"You sang harmony? On 'Farmer in the Dell'?"

"I'm sorry," Duncan said. "I thought it would help."

"Good lord," was all I could say. Then I laughed. Duncan had sung in choirs all his life, and I could imagine his resounding voice meeting those of the overburdened mothers. But then a worry registered: The other mothers would likely glare at me when I returned the following week. The jig was up: I was married to a freak, a derelict, a bum, or perhaps a eunuch. What other man would arrive utterly unkempt at a "parents and me" class on a Tuesday at 10 A.M.? Moreover, I was a double freak to have sent my husband, rather than to have shown up dutifully myself.

I began to realize, at that moment, that I might have a hard time making friends at Gymboree. Not just because there was circus music blaring whenever we weren't singing at the top of our lungs or because we had to manipulate our babies through no fewer than twelve "boogie stations" in a quick twenty minutes before the parachute finale began. No, I may not be able to strike up a Gymboree-based friendship because I hated the premise on which I felt the class was based. The premise, as I saw it, was that good mothers were solely responsible for their children's care during weekday work hours, and that these hours needed to be filled with developmentally appropriate and intellectually stimulating activities— stimulating for the child, that is. The mothers' minds could apparently turn to jelly for all the Miss Kimmys of the world cared.

I was back at work three months after that first Gymboree class, but I still felt compelled over the next three years to take Joseph or Ben to approximately twenty sessions of Kindermusik, four sing-alongs at the library, fifteen sessions of Monday morning at the Children's

Museum, two La Leche League meetings, eight story times at the library, four story times at local bookstores, and two hundred different visits to the park. It took me a while to catch on, but over time I began to realize that I was always at least a smidgen demoralized, angry, and out of sorts when I was alone with my children at any event comprised solely of other white mothers alone with their kids. I knew I was conflating, but I couldn't separate the women from the setting. How is it possible to be critical of a social situation while simultaneously open and compassionate to the people there? I have yet to figure this out, and my failure has hurt my ability to make friends with other mothers, certainly those I've encountered who are alone with their children at some point during the workweek, as I've been.

What made me go to as many Mom-and-me events as I did? To a certain extent, I believed the flyers and baby books, believed my young children needed enrichment and socialization. Also, I needed a break in the time I was with them, some outing around which to organize ourselves. The way a whole day with young children can slip through your hands without your being able to point to one concrete thing you did demoralized me. It's hard to fully describe this slippage to nonparents. What did you do today?, someone might ask, and it's hard to respond precisely: I changed seven diapers; answered ninety-two questions; made six snacks; wiped up fifty-six Cheerios, four smudges of jelly, and three bread crusts. And that was before 11 A.M.

Going to a Mom-and-me activity was, for me, like hiring a clown for a birthday party. It sounded better than it was, but it did take off some of the pressure of entertaining, of filling time.

Certainly one of my primary objectives was to be around other women, to—hopefully—make friends with them. As I coaxed my children into the car for yet another Mommy-and-me event (Ben and Joseph were often reluctant, not wanting to stop the play they were already engaged in), I kept thinking, This one will be different, it will be better than Gymboree. When it wasn't, I still continued to go sometimes, partly out of incredulity. That woman used to be a D.A.! That woman headed a recording studio! I'd been the director of a powerful grassroots organization. And look at us now—forcing our babies' hands to clap along to "If You're Happy and You Know It" while Clownie Jill danced on a stage below us with such overdramatization that her orange rag wig kept falling off.

The bleachers in the Children's Museum auditorium above Clownie Jill were packed with women and their toddlers—approximately sixty pair. *Which ones really were happy and they knew it? How many missed what they used to do on Monday mornings? Did anybody besides me view the change as a demotion while believing she also now knew a deeper kind of love?*

I never asked these questions to the fellow moms I met in class. I couldn't figure out how. These were virtual strangers, after all, and I didn't want to insult anyone, to make them think my own friend-o-meter was ticking away. Instead, we chatted on the curb about where a secondhand stroller could be had, which bottles were most like the breast, which pediatricians had office hours

on Sundays. Or else I passed these opportunities by saying nothing at all.

I would have liked to have interviewed these mothers—writing this book eventually gave me a justification
for doing precisely that—but during the first five years of
motherhood before I started the book, I couldn't always
convince myself that I was an observer, a social scientist.
This was my life, after all; it wasn't a research trip. Still,
the anthropologist persona I could slip into, if only in my
mind, struck me as eerily apropos. I could be at a sing-
along just blocks from my own home and feel distinctly
like I was in a different country from the one I'd lived in
before motherhood—a country hostile to women, yet
chock-full of us.

During the time when Ben was seven to nineteen
months old and Joseph was three-and-a-half to four-and-
a-half, I went to almost no mothering events. I couldn't
make myself go. It was as if I were on strike. Against
what, exactly? I believed in spending time with my children, and I wanted to. I believed in neighbors, in talking
to other women, in volunteering at my child's preschool,
in not routinely working sixteen-hour days away from
home. I even believed in—and enjoyed—singing. What I
didn't believe in was the uniformity of women doing
these things while men were at work. I took on a rather
stubborn stance: If these are the rules, then I won't play. I
can't; it's too infuriating. I'll take care of my kids (at home
alone) and I'll work (at home alone), with the brief exception of teaching my classes at the university.

I was often lonely, but my loneliness was far more
acute in group settings with other mothers and children.

As Vivian Gornick puts it, "It's easier actually to be alone than to be in the presence of that which arouses the need but fails to address it."*

The nature of the need was clear to me: intimate, uninterrupted talk with women, just like I'd had in abundance before marriage and motherhood. Ideally, a good bit of this talk would take place with other new mothers. *What had happened to us? How could we live as mothers and individuals at the same time? How could we best negotiate the twin pulls of work in the world and caring for our children?* I yearned for a mother-friend I could lie in bed with for hours on end until we could figure it out.

Up until Joseph was three-and-a-half and Ben was seven months old, I kept expecting, hoping, the chats beside the jungle gym would lead somewhere more intimate and substantive. Duncan and I had moved from our suburban rental house to a house at the center of an old neighborhood, rife with young families, precisely because we thought it would be a good place to make friends. Our house was at the very center of this neighborhood— directly across the street from a park. All I had to do on any given day was go across the street to be surrounded by women—women on leave from doctoral programs, women who'd been crime reporters, women who'd directed arts organizations, women who'd biked across the country. Surely I could make one intimate friend in this setting.

In the past, I'd eagerly sought out all-women enclaves and events. I'd hosted all-women dinner parties, taken

---

* Vivian Gornick, *Approaching Eye Level* (Boston: Beacon, 1996), p. 136.

part in feminist reading groups, gone on road trips with female friends. None of these women-only occasions had functioned to let men off the hook of anything, though. On the contrary, it was pro-woman, I thought, to drive around Alabama visiting folk artists with two girlfriends. Being at the park day after day while your husband was at work didn't strike me as pro-woman. I was having a very hard time doing this myself, to the part-time extent I was doing it, and I felt worse—rather than comforted—when I was surrounded by other mothers on similar, or even less equitable, schedules.

The way we were always harried and distracted didn't help my assessment of the situation at the park. Our children would be dangling precariously from the monkey bars or jumping fearlessly into the deep end of the pool, we had shopping to do, people were bound to have hunger meltdowns soon and we'd forgotten to pack enough snacks. I'd never enjoyed multitasking—or chatting, for that matter—and I was at a loss as to how even to try and make the park conversations more substantive, to make my time there less demoralizing in terms of adult social interaction.

When two of us mothers would attempt real conversation—for example, when the wife of one of Duncan's colleagues and I managed to exchange about eight sentences on Spanish feminism and psychoanalysis beside the sandbox as our one- and two-year-olds played—I was so happy and excited, and then so disappointed when we inevitably had to cut it short. Would it have been better—or at least less painful—never to have tried? Think of the sexual analogy: If your male partner always comes quickly then rolls over, you might just get to the point where sex doesn't seem worth it.

Of course rather than giving up on sex, it's infinitely more optimistic, take-charge, and can-do American to go to sex therapy, take up with a better lover, or read a sex manual then try again with some mood music and candles. I did try all of these moves—or rather, their friendship analogies—in my pursuit of mother-friends.

Fortunately, I hadn't been an utter failure on the friend-making front since Joseph's birth. I'd made three close girlfriends in that time; they just weren't mothers. Each of these women was younger than I was, a writer, and someone who reminded me, in some way, of who I'd been. There was Petra, a funny, intellectual, and feminist graduate student in UT's English department; Miriam, a staunchly supportive friend and extremely ambitious short story writer; and Felicity, a gifted photographer and poet. All three had boisterous, irreverent selves, and I felt like myself when I was with them. Our relationships were based solidly in intimate talk, just as my friendships with women had always been.

I told details about my children to my new friends—how Ben said "Uh-oh" for every pinecone on the ground, how Joseph performed magic "experiences" with pots and water, how Ben twirled my hair as he drank milk from his sippy cup just as he'd done when he'd been nursing. And I talked about the less idyllic aspects of motherhood as well—how upset I was about the postlactation diminishment of my breasts, how angry I occasionally was at Duncan, how tired I was, how much childbirth had hurt. Petra, Miriam, and Felicity were deeply interested, in part because they might choose motherhood themselves, and I was their peephole to the other side. Primarily, though, they simply enjoyed the freakish, the human, and the complicated just as I did, just as Christine, Vicky, and all of my old friends did.

I loved hearing details about my new friends' work, partners, parents, and siblings, as well. The particularities of a woman's life, especially as articulated by someone bright and funny, were endlessly interesting to me. In short, my relationships with Petra, Miriam, and Felicity matched perfectly with my understanding of what women friends could and should be. Because of the demands of motherhood, and less so of my work, I couldn't always talk to my new friends as long or as frequently as I wanted to, but I worked hard to make time for these friendships. They were a lifeline to me. Meanwhile, I kept doggedly trying to make mother-friends—even during the year when I was on strike against the park.

I tried socializing with full-time working mothers, primarily Duncan's female colleagues. Perhaps this setup was less than perfect from the outset. *Well, welcome to the real world,* I told myself. *There's no match.com for a best mother-friend. Get out there and be friendly to all the mothers you can find!* At Duncan's departmental potlucks, I felt embarrassed, though, that I only had a part-time job at the same university where these women had tenure-track positions. Several times I corrected female (and male) colleagues of Duncan's who assumed I'd dropped out of graduate school to have children. "I dropped out years before I got pregnant," I would say. "I dropped out to work in politics." This was true, but I didn't like the way I felt so driven to say it, to be absolutely sure that no one thought I'd taken the mommy track to part-time work. They could think I'd taken any other indecisive or compromised route, just not that one.

Basically, I was afraid that Duncan's female colleagues looked down on me. If there were a totem pole of power, professional women were at the top, part-time working mothers and artistic types were somewhere in the middle, and stay-at-home mothers were at the bottom. I felt certain that everyone believed this was the way the pole stacked. Of course the selflessness pole stacked the opposite way with stay-at-home mothers at the top and professional women at the bottom. I appreciated being at neither pole's tail end, but I also felt like I was getting slammed from both sides.

Many women seemed to bend over backward, though, *not* to come across as judging, despite whatever they might be thinking to themselves. When one of Duncan's colleagues, who was eight months pregnant with her first child when I was six months pregnant with Ben, asked what I heard as "What do you do?" while we both sipped cranberry juice and seltzer on the couch, I was delighted. We were at the chair of the history department's house, and young children raced around us while several historians tried to talk shop nearby, above the fray. I started to tell Duncan's colleague, Andrea, about an article I was writing on magic, but she looked perplexed.

"I said, 'When are you due?' " she clarified.

"Oh," I laughed, "I thought you said 'What do you do?' "

Looking extremely nervous, she said, "Oh, no, I would never ask a mother that."

Even though I had been thrilled to have—or rather, think I had—Andrea's interest in my life beyond family, I knew exactly why she denied the question so adamantly. It could be offensive or hurtful to ask a pregnant woman with a young child what she "did," implying that the questioner thought she needed to do something beyond mothering. It could enrage a stay-at-home mother or make her feel diminished. *Didn't people know how hard she worked from sunup to midnight every day? The gall to ask what she "did"!*

I could see that "What do you do?" was a dicey question for mothers of young children, as were many of the questions I myself had refrained from asking mothers I didn't know well: *Does it bother you that you do 90 percent of the childcare? Do you ever want to wring your husband's neck when he asks where the salt is? Do you miss the job you had at twenty-eight so much that it keeps you up some nights?* If myriad questions were off-limits in a conversation with a mother you were just meeting, though—and I thought I could see why some of my proposed questions should be—then how were you supposed to proceed toward friendship? How could you possibly build a friendship if "What do you do?"—the most basic of getting-to-know-you questions—was taboo? Becoming friends with other mothers was beginning to seem like an absolute minefield to me.

I knew I should have more chutzpah and confidence with Duncan's colleagues and less judgment and fear toward the mothers in the park. But like all of these women, I had so little time and so many demands. This was probably the one common denominator every single one of us shared. Given the complications, pitfalls, and high likelihood of feeling judged, on the one hand, or making my conversational partner feel judged, on the other, it was no wonder that aggressively seeking out new mother-friends on a day when I was already incredibly pressed for time was rarely my highest priority.

Rachel Cusk talks about the way, as a mother, it always feels that there's a taxi meter running.* *Forty-five minutes left until the baby-sitter leaves, thirty minutes until bedtime when I can go back to work, six minutes to take a shower before* Wishbone *ends, seventeen minutes before I have to get in the car for preschool pickup.* Times when I invited another mother out to lunch at the Mexican restaurant around the corner from my house—often a mother who worked part-time and primarily from home as I did—I couldn't help but glance frequently at the fluorescent clock with sombreros in place of numbers. I'd think to myself: *Well, that digression about summer camp was enjoyable, but was it really worth $15 because that's how much it cost, in terms of childcare for two children.* Or I'd think: *Was this entire lunch, pleasant as it was, really worth an hour of my time in a day when I only have four hours to work?*

Often the answer I came to was a brutal *no.* If I couldn't be certain in advance that a particular lunch date would lead to intimacy, then I often didn't feel I could afford the time. I was aware that this was a ludicrous thought, that friendships didn't develop efficiently; nor could they be predicted ahead of time. Still, I couldn't stop the calculations. The only way to avoid this kind of pressure was to

---

* Rachel Cusk, *A Life's Work* (New York: Picador, 2001).

force my friend-making time to coincide with my mom-on-duty time, a thought that sent me right back to the park with all its conversational obstacles.

Were other mothers having the friendship difficulties I was? A woman whom I'd met in prenatal yoga and now saw very occasionally at nonpregnant yoga commented to another mother and me a year after her son had been born: "I've made so many new girlfriends as a mother! It's a bonus I never expected."

"That hasn't been my experience at all," I replied sheepishly, picking imaginary lint off my sticky mat.

Which park did she frequent? I asked her and took my children there dozens of times. More to the point—and I did not ask her this—what was I doing wrong?

I did ask Duncan this question. I asked him that night as we folded laundry and listened to Stevie Wonder.

"Don't take this the wrong way," he said, "but people often perceive you as hostile."

"Me—hostile?" I said with a tinge of hostility in my voice. "What do you mean?"

"Well, people don't always realize that you're joking when you say something dark."

"I'm not always joking."

"Well, people don't like that, focusing on the dark. They've all had hard days like we have. They probably just want to relax, talk about something positive—or at least neutral."

"Like what? What neutral things do most people want to talk about? Butterflies? Fucking seagulls?"

"See what I mean? See how hostile you are?"

I could, in fact, see. Just recently, I'd been breast-feeding six-month-old Ben in a floral armchair at Joseph's preschool, pretty irritated that I hadn't been able to make it home without nursing, when another mother came up to me and asked brightly, "How long do you breast-feed your children?"

"As long as I can stand it," popped out of my mouth. I don't think my tone was hostile, per se, and I distinctly remember smiling warmly at her, just after my remark. But she made a quick exit anyway, practically racing out of the bright purple door with her eighteen-month-old in tow.

On the one hand, I was simply telling the truth. Was my truth that horrifying to her? Delving deeper, though, I had to admit that I suspected her question was begging for an ideological answer, something like, "I always nurse my children through their twenty-fourth month." I knew she was breast-feeding her toddler, and I thought she might be looking for a comrade-in-arms, or breasts. Where was the harm in that, though? Why shouldn't she try to bond with me around breast-feeding?

I realized I might have been snippy, despite my conciliatory smile, because I feared she was a lactivist, one of the sizable group of Austin mothers who rather militantly, from my perspective, advocated long-term breast-feeding. I could almost pass muster with these women; I'd nursed Joseph for fourteen months, but I wasn't at all sure I'd be able to make it that long with Ben. We'd started giving Ben formula within weeks of his birth, and I'd never gotten more hostile looks in my life than I did when bottle-feeding Ben in public in Austin. *Look at her; she's poisoning her child. It's such a shame when mothers are too selfish to nurse.*

Of course I could have been dead wrong about the reason for the hostile glances. Maybe the women who stared disapprovingly as I bottle-fed Ben—and it happened on numerous occasions, with a different set of women each time—took offense at Ben's hat, my uncombed hair, whatever shirt I was wearing, or our brand of diaper bag. In any event, none of this history necessarily had any bearing on Melissa, the mom who approached me at the preschool. I had no idea if she was a lactivist! I was judging her—and surely that judgment seeped into the tone of my response—because I believed she was *judging me*, subjecting my breast-feeding plans to her friend-o-meter. But what if she wasn't? What if she was just curious?

Truth be told, by the time Ben was seven months old and Joseph was three-and-a-half, I didn't believe other mothers were capable of curiosity without judgment because I had become utterly incapable of it myself. My mind had grown petty, full of hundreds of minute observations—cloth or paper diapers, PBS or no TV at all, a firm bedtime or up all night, Avent or Playtex bottles, Snugli or sling. Sometimes I simply noted these distinctions, but often I registered some kind of judgment. Either way, it took up an enormous amount of mental energy.

What had happened to me? I was ashamed of myself! I'd always been one of the big-picture folks, the person to ask the "why" questions. There was no room at all for existential musing or probing critiques of American life now. My brain was chock-full of minutiae. I'd become the monitor of petty details, the queen of judgment, and it was poisoning my life. My own evaluative small-mindedness caused me far more distress, actually, than whatever judgments I perceived as coming at me from other mothers. One thing was perfectly clear: It was no wonder I couldn't make any mother-friends. I'd become hypercritical on the one hand, and possibly paranoid on the other. Social hermithood seemed like a good interim plan until I could figure out how to stop judging and feeling judged.

Between April 1998 and April 1999, I rarely ventured out to the park, a preschool potluck, or a child's birthday party. Whenever I did, I'd come back so demoralized that Duncan soon saw it was better for our family if he handled as many public parenting situations as possible. He took Joseph to preschool nearly every day, and he went to all the birthday parties. For almost a year, I was Mommy Private, and he was Mommy Public.

I also had trouble in grocery stores during that time—especially fancy ones. Some days, it depressed me beyond repair to see mothers buying overpriced vegetables while their kids ate organic fruit leathers in an elaborate double-seated pushcart. It felt even worse to do it myself. Is this what it meant—at least in Austin—to be a mother with a stake in the larger world? Perhaps these other mother-shoppers were working at night via the Internet to expose corrupt business executives. I certainly wasn't. I suspected that for some of the mother-shoppers at least, as was the case for me on the days when I wasn't teaching, their most frequent engagement with the world was as consumers. I didn't want myself or my family to starve, but there were a good many days when I literally couldn't stomach myself as buyer-for-the-nuclear-family, especially not at Whole Foods. I liked organic field greens as much as the next yuppie, but for almost a year, I could hardly go into stores where they were sold. There was so much alarmist propaganda—on the walls, on the packaging, in the crunchy magazines by the checkout—and it all seemed pointed at mothers. *Buy this! Wash this! Cook with this, and your children will be safe.* I simply couldn't keep up with all the toxins.

I took to sneaking across the highway to McDonald's where the playground was considerably more diverse than the one outside Austin's premier supermarket, and where it was unlikely that I'd run into anyone I knew. Certainly there was no mention of toxins. I drank decaf, which seemed harmless enough, while Joseph and Ben raced happily around the elaborate and spiffy wooden playscape. Being at McDonald's was an oasis to me, a break from the judgment I'd come to feel near constantly in my own neighborhood. Who could judge me here? We were at McDonald's, for God's sake, the place where parents—by definition—are just trying to get by.

Some would argue that it's a sign that something is gravely wrong when McDonald's is the place you go not to be depressed. Indeed, I knew I was on shaky ground, and this is when I began seeing Louise, my then-therapist. Louise and I spent a lot of our initial sessions talking about why I hadn't made any friends who were mothers during the three and a half years since Joseph had been born. Sure, there were neighborhood mothers I was friendly with, but there were no mothers in town I talked deeply and intimately with, no one like Chris.

Louise told me what I already knew, that it was inadequate to keep talking on the phone to my "real" friends

(Louise made quotation marks in the air with her fingers at this point) who lived in New York, San Francisco, Detroit, Berlin, and Santa Fe while refusing to try harder with mothers-in-the-flesh at the park. "You need friends who are mothers," she said, "and they need to live in Austin." I couldn't have agreed more. But I was mother-phobic.

Here's how I saw the situation: My sense of self felt so thin and frayed that I was afraid of losing it altogether. As a necessary survival step, I needed to do things and go places that buoyed me, or at least didn't assault me. Ideally, I needed to surround myself with people who had strong senses of self. If I couldn't readily find any adult women like this, I'd best stay home alone in my limited spare time, reading words written by strong selves or talking on the phone to old friends—or new single friends—who reminded me of who I'd been.

I was able to go out with my children—I just couldn't take them to places frequented by other mothers and children, except McDonald's. Instead of the park, Joseph, Ben, and I went to near-deserted museums where we lay on our stomachs and drew what we saw, we went to twenty-something coffeehouses and played our own version of chess on the built-in boards (Ben chewed on the knights), and we went to abandoned parking lots to ride bikes and scooters.

Something to do with motherhood was causing me trouble, but as long as I managed to work at least a few hours a day, it wasn't time spent with my children. When one of them was crying or whining, certainly I felt stress, but for the most part, my children were an enormous ballast. Their joy was infectious, and as long as I didn't have to see other mothers, I usually felt just fine.

Apparently, I had a social sickness, and I tried hard to describe its nature to Louise, who sat rather stony faced on a beige leather couch as I talked. Beside her was a round table that she'd littered with conchs. "Shells are like bones," my sister, Celia, always said. "It's morbid to collect them." I tried to overlook Louise's potential shell fetish and to focus, instead, on the problem at hand, the one I was paying her to help me solve: I was afraid of other mothers, and yet I was a mother.

I told Louise that the good mothers, in particular, scared me. I was referring to the women I perceived as meeting new-millennial expectations for good mother-hood: long-term breast-feeding, no work during children's preschool years, ferrying children to several enriching activities per week, infrequent use of baby-sitters. The women who did these things projected a kind of selfless-ness that I found frightening. Where had their selves gone? If I hung around with them, would my self disappear as well? I was already slipping, and it felt quite dangerous to be with women who may have slipped even further, as if I'd recently given up smoking then chose to hang out solely with inveterate chain-smokers. Was it love that was goading these women on? Could an absence of self possi-bly be loving, could it be good for children?

I'd read psychoanalytic theories that argued the con-trary. In Jessica Benjamin's *The Bonds of Love* she writes that what children need from parents, above all, is recog-nition, and it doesn't count for the child if it comes from a compromised self. Recognition feels good only when it comes from someone with a full and strong self. If Benjamin was right, I told Louise, then one of the best things I could do for myself—and thereby my children—was to stay away from other mothers who seemed to have turned their lives over to motherhood. If what they had was contagious—and I feared it was—I really didn't want to catch it.

I suspected that maternal selflessness spread via guilt. I could read all the feminist theory I could carry home from the library and still feel a stab of guilt if I passed a woman holding her baby and watching her toddler in the sandbox while my children were home with a baby-sitter.

Louise hadn't read Jessica Benjamin, but she could get the gist, she said, from what I'd told her. Everything I was saying and reading was so extreme, she said. Could all the women at the park really be selfless?

"No," I said, "but they're striving for it. The atmosphere is very competitive out there."

"Perhaps you're the competitive one," Louise returned. "Haven't you always been competitive?"

"I guess," I said. I picked up one of the worry stones in the pink bowl Louise kept beside the client chair and began to worry it around and around in my hand.

I didn't want to tell Louise how obsessively I noticed all the minutiae about a woman's mothering—how long she breast-fed, how much childcare she used, what her children ate, where they slept, if they watched TV. I didn't want to tell her that this information went, rather competitively, into my selfless-o-meter. Was a given woman more selfless than I was? If she was, I usually felt guilty, I often felt anger toward a society and a husband that would make her feel compelled to act this way, and I almost always felt empathy and concern for her as well. I knew Louise would tell me to focus on the empathy and "move beyond" the anger and guilt. I also knew she wouldn't be able to tell me how.

I felt I could see my bind clearly: Guilt, anger, and a desire not to appear judgmental crippled my ability to speak to other mothers with compassion, to ask genuinely how they were managing. Instead I'd try to chat as value-neutrally as I could (a kind of talk I'd always hated), or else I'd say nothing, neither of which advanced the friendship.

I did have a friend-o-meter as well, but it was looking for radically different qualities than my selfless-o-meter. Was this woman irreverent? Unflinching, possibly, in her use of the word "fuck"? Was she anything but a perfectionist? Did she have strong passions beyond her family—skiing, making jewelry, playing the cello? Did her partner, if she had one, do a hefty share of the housework and parenting? Was she willing to take care of herself, to go out every once in a while and kick up her heels?

As I felt my own self slipping through stress, sleep deprivation, lack of time, interruption, an utterly demoralizing amount of laundry, and the corrosive effects of constant guilt, I was looking more than ever for friends with rock-solid selves, boisterous women like those I'd always loved—women who could shore me up and inspire me to greater levels of self-acceptance rather than stir up anxieties that tended to cause even more self-doubt. My friend-o-meter was, in fact, a near opposite of my selfless-o-meter.

I must have been nuts—or at least shockingly naïve— to have ever thought that good mothers and good friends would share the same qualities. From what I could tell, the closer someone came to the contemporary definition of good motherhood, the less available she was as a friend. If a woman was selfless, after all, who was there left to be friends with?

I conveyed this analysis to Louise (minus the details about what petty observations I made of other mothers), and she was not impressed. If I was afraid of other mothers, if I thought they didn't make good friends, that was simply a form of self-hatred. I needed to look within and see why I hated myself.

It's self-protection! I nearly shrieked.

It's self-hatred, she reiterated.

We were at loggerheads yet again.

After six months, I "prematurely terminated" with Louise, which meant she still thought I had serious problems when I left. I quit, though, because she was making me crazy. I actually agreed with several of Louise's insights—she had me pegged accurately as competitive, long before motherhood; and I knew I needed to think about the degree to which I felt self-disgust at an event like Gymboree, then chose to project it out on other women. But Louise and I would never see eye-to-eye because she continually dismissed the role of culture. In her book, everything was always caused by, and capable of being solved by, the individual. It was textbook shrink thought, and I didn't like it. I didn't want to monolithically blame "The Man" for my woes, but surely some of what I was perceiving in terms of pressure on mothers to be selfless came from life in a sexist world. Similarly, a good chunk of the mother-to-mother judgmentalism I sensed had to be related to America's competitive, consumerist ethos. What ancient "I'm OK, you're OK" mentality was Louise living in that she couldn't face these facts? While we had battled about the role of culture throughout our therapy, I didn't tell her directly that her refusal to accept it was why I was leaving. I just said I planned to pursue "other avenues" for healing.

A few months later, I briefly saw a religious counselor I dubbed "Mr. Truth" because an Episcopal priest and friend of mine had told me, "Scott will look you in the eye and make you tell the truth." Now this was what I wanted someone to do—make me speak the truth, the one truth. I could see so many truths, some of which blamed me for my unhappiness and lack of mother-friends, others that pointed the finger elsewhere.

When I told Scott about the mothers at the park, how their projected selflessness scared me and also made me guilty, he said, "Of course. It's a terrible thing our culture does to mothers. Don't waste any more time trying to make friends at the park. You need to hang around with artists—other writers and painters."

Yes! It was so relieving to have my perspective affirmed, perhaps particularly by someone so different from me: a sixty-five-year-old male religious adviser. And also, no. I *was* a mother—should I just shuck my children off and pretend not to be, frequenting Austin's trendier bars, galleries, and poetry slams by myself? I did do a fair amount of this after Scott's advice, and the outings to smoky cafés where people younger than I raged against their parents did occasionally lift my spirits. Austin was full of ranters—some of them very, very good. But none of this slam-watching addressed my desire for mother-friends. There were no mothers of young children in the house.

When some mothers in my neighborhood asked if I wanted to help start a book group, I jumped at the chance. If we could just be alone together (leaving our husbands in charge at home, thereby quelling the how-much-is-this-costing meter), we might get down to some real talking! Certainly I'd be happy to talk about books. I loved books. I hoped we'd pick some books about motherhood—juicy ones, controversial ones we could debate—and I said as much. No one else in our group of eight seemed immediately keen on the idea.

"I definitely don't want to limit our reading to books by women," Carla said. "I did that in another group, and it was very repetitive."

I couldn't see how Sappho, Simone de Beauvoir, and Toni Morrison, say, could possibly be viewed as repetitive, but I was no reading separatist. I read—and enjoyed—something by a male author nearly every day. "That's fine with me," I said cheerily. "I didn't mean to suggest anything limiting."

A few months later when it was my turn to select our material, people had expressed an interest in poetry, so I handed out a sheaf of poems by Kate Daniels, Audre Lorde, Adrienne Rich, and Sharon Olds—almost all of the poems about motherhood, and many about breast-feeding. We never actually had a meeting to discuss these poems (the following meeting was canceled because so many people were out of town), but when I did ask the group two months later what they'd thought of the poems, there was a brief silence. Then Debra, who currently had a five-year-old and a nine-year-old, said, "That time with an infant was so awful. I don't want to think about it at all. I'm just glad it's over."

Now this was fascinating! Maybe nobody other than me could even bear to talk about motherhood. Certainly Debra's comment shed new light for me on the books we'd been reading so far: mostly novels, many set in faraway places like Africa, Indonesia, or the sci-fi future. Some featured heroines more daring than any of us were; others chronicled the adventures of alienated male loners who traveled back roads with a dog. Perhaps book group was largely a way to escape from our current lives for a few hours a month—through reading about experiences widely divergent from our own, as well as literally being absent from family life once a month at a meeting of other women. Just because this hadn't been my agenda didn't mean it wasn't a good one.

Actually, when my attendance at book group grew rather spotty during my year of hermithood, Debra said, with a hint of cattiness, "Faulkner hasn't been here since we switched to Thursday nights because she can't stand to miss *ER*." I realized she was right, at least partially. Who was I to question other women's escapism? I loved the gorgeous and high-powered doctors making harrowing decisions and having complex interracial relationships. Take me away from my prosaic Texas life, oh great nighttime drama!

What I had wanted from book group, though, was something different, something more along the lines of consciousness-raising. The fact that book group was not

consciousness-raising had as much to do with my inter-
mittent attendance as did my obsession with *ER*.

Every American woman I know is in a book group. Book
groups are to the new millennium what consciousness-
raising was—in certain neighborhoods—for the 1970s. Call
me anachronistic, but I realized, as I thought about my book
group, that I was hungry for some old-fashioned CR.

I wanted to talk directly about selfhood and motherhood, about loving your kids but also loving yourself, and
I was hoping book group would include books on these
subjects as a springboard to discussion. I still wanted to
figure out, with other mothers, what had happened to us,
what motherhood meant, and how we could best live as
mothers without losing ourselves.

In her 1976 memoir, *The Mother Knot* (a book I couldn't
persuade our book group to read), Jane Lazarre quotes the
leaflet she and a friend handed out in their New Haven
housing complex:

> Tired of being somebody's mother or somebody's wife?
> Come to Jean Rosenthal's house on Monday night. Talk
> about your real feelings. Women's group forming.*

I wanted to get this leaflet! I wanted to go to Jean
Rosenthal's house on Monday night! While I'd never been
in a consciousness-raising group, per se, I had always
talked about my life—starting, actually, circa 1976—and

---

* Jane Lazarre, *The Mother Knot* (Durham, N.C.: Duke University Press,
  1997), p. 64. Originally published in 1976 by McGraw-Hill Book
  Company.

listened intently as other women talked about theirs. This was how a life made sense; this was how a woman knew who she was. It was simply too much to expect her to do it on her own or with the help, only, of a male partner, however loving and astute he was. Why did it feel like I couldn't find any mothers who wanted to share this kind of talk with me now? Could motherhood, itself, have shut us up?

I thought of a conversation I'd had with my oldest friend, Vicky, eight years prior. It had taken place in December 1991, the first time I'd seen Vicky since I'd started dating Duncan. She'd asked what he was like.

"He's great," I said, "warm, sensitive, funny—I can't wait for you to meet him."

"How's the sex?"

"Good, really good."

Vicky stopped in her tracks to look at me. We were on the Upper West Side of Manhattan, a few blocks from her apartment, and snow was falling fast and heavy so it was particularly striking that she would stop walking. We were both freezing and eager to get inside.

"You're going to marry him, aren't you?" she said.

"I think so," I replied even though Duncan and I had been dating only five months, and marriage had never been broached.

"I'm so happy for you!" Vicky said, and she gave me a huge smile.

I knew she hadn't predicted our wedding based on the few words I'd said about Duncan. Her assumption came much more from what I didn't say, how I didn't dish. I didn't give one detail about his penis, for example. With previous boyfriends, I'd told Vicky about a certain crookedness or surprising lack of circumcision. Certainly, I didn't say that Duncan could twirl a Frisbee on his penis, a fact Chris had once conveyed about one of her beaus.

I was withholding details because I had something sacred and private to withhold, and Vicky was able to sniff out the meaning of my reticence in an instant. If I wasn't going to be completely forthright about my sex life anymore—with an elaborate panoply of lurid details intact—could she and I still be good friends? I thought so, and I hoped Vicky did as well, but the shift was a very real one. Becoming relatively close-mouthed about a man who would become my husband was the first step, I realized in retrospect, on a path that led me—and other women to an even larger degree, from what I could tell—to the acute silence I was hearing and participating in as a wife and mother.

✳✳✳

Eight years later in Austin, there was even more at stake in my married and maternal life, more to feel allegiance to, even as I—and I couldn't be the only one—felt conflicted about much of it. I wanted to talk to women, like I always had, but my sense of association was different now. It wasn't just me and my girlfriends against the world of men, expecting (partially) to be hurt and dissed by them, but still hoping to find one to love. This battle had been the food of conversation for years. Now I'd found a man, I loved him deeply, and he and I had made two others. This man and these boys were my tribe now. I was like Romeo after he leaves his friends behind to go love and die with Juliet.

Hold up with the epic analogies, I told myself. Why should signing on, or ending up, in a house-man-child arrangement mean losing intimacy with female friends? I hadn't lost the possibility of intimacy with my old friends, or my new friends who weren't mothers. There had unquestionably been some painful showdowns, though—the time Chris said I was "settling" by marrying Duncan, forcing a happy ending when life was a lot more complicated than that; or the time in the coffee shop when Renata told me with unflinching candor that she felt betrayed that I planned to move to North Carolina with Duncan. "I thought we were going to move to New Orleans together," she said. "That's what we've always talked about."

I'd been on the other side as well. I took to calling myself "the bad daughter" during my senior year in college when my three roommates, all happily paired, wouldn't go clubbing with me, instead opting to stay in with their boyfriends. "Where've you been? Who'd you sleep with?" they'd half-joke to me in the morning. It was lonely, and I missed them, as well as being jealous of what they had.

All of these friends and I talked directly—eventually—when it felt like a man or men were separating us from one another, and we worked hard to make that not be the case. Changes took place—I've now spent more nights with Duncan than with any woman—but I still sleep comfortably beside Chris and Celia.

The mothers in my Austin neighborhood and I didn't have any history of intimacy. We didn't necessarily want one another—women we saw nearly every day at the park, preschool pickup, the grocery store, the coffee shop, the pool—to know about the strife in our marriages or the frustration we felt toward a willful child. We certainly didn't feel free to talk about these feelings when our children could be listening, which was almost always. But we weren't less than forthcoming with one another just because children were listening. We wanted to appear that we were managing everything just fine, that we were, in fact, good and competent mothers with stable and loving marriages. We felt, I believe, that any negative comment a woman made about her domestic situation could be perceived by other mothers as a lack of motherly love. No mother I've ever met—myself included—has wanted this rap.

The level of reticence was new ground for me. What about the tiny inconsistencies that needed to be poked and prodded, the injustices, the way things didn't add up, the daily furors and frustrations? These were the very meat of conversation, in my view, yet I could hardly make any headway when I broached any of this regarding our current maternal lives with other mothers. Sure, people would complain about their mothers or mothers-in-law, but what about how they were feeling, right now, in their own houses? Unless a woman was literally bursting with anger, as Colleen had been when she'd run Duncan and me down in the street to tell us how pissed she was at her husband, Richard, for not doing any housework, then a woman might not talk at all. To me, it felt like a near-stonewall on conversation.

✳✳✳

Vicky had her first child two years after I did. She called me when he was two months old, and I was four months pregnant with Ben. We chatted a bit, and then she almost whispered, "Do you ever dream of going to the hospital?"

"I do," I said immediately. " I wouldn't mind the bad food on trays. I'd take one of those trays right now—I'm really hungry."

"Would you even eat the lime Jell-O?"

"I would. My mother used to make it when I had a sore throat. I wish someone would make me some now."

"I'd be so happy to be taken care of," Vicky said, "just for one day, even. I wouldn't mind if I had to have an IV. Would you mind an IV?"

"Not a bit. What's one little prick in the arm?"

"Would you even go to a mental hospital?" Vicky pursued.

"I'd go to one of the fancy ones. I could just lie in bed and read. Can you imagine anything better?"

"Don't they take away your books at mental hospitals?"

"God, I hope not. How else could you get well?"

"People might be screaming. It might be hard to sleep."

"Joseph screams now," I said.

Vicky didn't say anything for a few seconds. "Faulkner," she then began, "is there something wrong with us that we're fantasizing about going to a mental hospital?"

I was quick to reassure. "I don't think so. I really don't. I just think we're very, very tired."

"I don't know how much longer I can live like this," Vicky said.

"Me, either," I agreed.

208 ✳ Faulkner Fox

***

You don't cop to being so desperate for rest that you're envious of life in an insane asylum to just anyone. I didn't need—or expect—this level of honesty with everyone in my neighborhood. But I needed a lot more, on a daily basis, than I was getting. Without it, I felt like a ghost or a faker in my own life.

I started to write about my experiences of motherhood out of loneliness, initially. Soon thereafter, I began interviewing other mothers. I explained that I was primarily writing a first-person narrative, but that I wanted to know how representative my experience had been or how idiosyncratic.

"You're interviewing for context," one sharp interviewee and professor put it.

"Yes, that's it exactly," I agreed.

I wasn't falsely representing myself—I was actually writing this book by the time I started interviewing mothers—and I did everything official: got signed release forms, told people to stop me if they ever felt uncomfortable or wanted something off-the-record. Still, I knew I was no sociologist. Given the kind of book I was writing, it was very unlikely that I would actually quote from an interview.

I was conducting interviews, partially, because I couldn't seem to get to the nitty-gritty of how women, with the exception of my old friends, felt about motherhood otherwise. I asked questions like: What's changed since you've become a mother? How do you and your partner figure out who does what in terms of housework and babycare? How much of your experience as a mother feels like a choice you've made and how much feels imposed? What do you like about being a mother? Are there things you dislike?

I got honest and full answers to these questions. I was so happy! If I had to construct myself as a social scientist in order to hear women talk truthfully about their lives, I'd do it every single day of my life.

Was this unethical? I hoped not. When I approached a potential interviewee, I explained as fully as I could about the book I was writing and then asked if she wanted to help me get a sense of how widespread my feelings were by telling me about her own experience of motherhood. Almost everyone responded with excitement. Afterward, the large majority said they'd enjoyed being interviewed.

"That was like free therapy!" one woman exclaimed.

"Thank you," I replied, assuming from her tone that she felt more positive about therapy than I currently did.

I did have some take-backs, though, something I'd never experienced in the many times I'd interviewed people on topics other than motherhood. Two women who saw me a few days after their interviews each asked me—partly joking, partly serious—not to use certain sections of what they'd said. "I think it could really damage my daughter to read that I feel this way," one of them added.

"I won't quote anything from your interview," I said immediately. "I don't want you to feel uncomfortable or worried at all." She seemed disappointed, but also relieved.

A third woman wrote me an extremely distressed e-mail the night after our interview, and when I quickly proffered the tape of our conversation, she took it, saying she planned to burn it.

I felt terrible. What had I done to these women? Had I brutally coerced them to say things they later sorely regretted? I told Petra about one interview in which a lesbian mother described herself as doing 85 percent of the childcare while her CEO partner worked, had dinner with friends, and occasionally drove around in the country alone. "If I was straight, I'd call our situation sexist," the woman had said.

"Given that you're a lesbian, what do you call it?" I'd pursued.

"Life," had been her response, and she said it as a question: "Life?"

When Petra heard this exchange, she laughed and then said, "You're not interviewing people, you're torturing them!"

"Should I stop?" I asked her anxiously. "Should I not ask such pointed questions?"

"No, no—you're fine," she reassured. "You've got to find out. You're writing a book."

I was, but my need for the interviews was much more than professional. I'd been itching to have this kind of conversation for five long years before I sat my first subject down. I needed to know if my feelings about motherhood were entirely unique: Was something wrong with me as an individual, or were certain aspects of my malaise more widespread?

From what I gathered from the interviews, there was

much overlap with my experience and much divergence. Whatever a woman said, it was incredibly relieving to have had the conversation. My attitude as I listened to these mothers talk was curious, thankful for their time, and almost entirely empathetic. I never felt judgmental. What an enormous respite from my own worst self! Most women also seemed to feel relieved after our interviews—many said as much. This definitely wasn't the case, though, for the woman who pledged to burn her tape.

It's my belief that the take-backs, the second thoughts a few of my interviewees had, were related to the same issue that made motherhood silencing: When a mother voices a complaint, critique, or frustration about her maternal life, she fears that this means she doesn't love her child enough. Or at best, it means that others will perceive her as not loving her child enough. The first thought (not loving your child enough) causes extreme guilt, and the second (that others will perceive you as unloving) causes extreme social anxiety. Either way, a woman can feel she'd better take back anything that spills forth rather recklessly in honesty, or else not say anything critical about motherhood at all.

After an interview, often my interviewees would want to know about my experiences, what had led me to be writing this book. "I've felt surprisingly isolated as a mother," I'd say. "I wanted to write something that would make other mothers feel less alone."

Thank you, I'd say. Thank you for sharing your experience with me. And thank you, especially, for making me feel less alone today.

POSTSCRIPT

I have several good mother-friends now. Some of them are the same women I had a hard time connecting with originally at the park, one is a colleague of Duncan's, others are single and divorced mothers. Friendship with the single and divorced mothers has often been smoother and quicker for me because when we choose to be together with one another and our children, I don't feel that any man is being let off the hook of anything. I tell Duncan to go somewhere else so I can be with my friend, and I know she isn't just passing time with me, chatting amiably enough, but only until it's time to start cooking for the returning breadwinner, the real enchilada in her life.

The process of becoming friends with married mothers, like me, has typically taken longer. Surprisingly and sadly long, which is why I felt compelled to write this chapter. One of the reasons for the length of time it's taken, I've decided, is pure circumstance. If it takes eight hours of honest, relatively focused conversation to begin to feel intimate with someone, I could easily accomplish that in a weekend when I was twenty-five. In my thirties, it could take two and a half years to accumulate eight hours of rich talk with another mother, and the fact that it came in five- to ten-minute snippets never felt as fulfilling to me as two four-hour marathons over wine and dinner would have.

I've also had to learn to change my expectations of friendship with other mothers. These friendships weren't going to be like my friendships prior to marriage and motherhood, and the sooner I stopped expecting them to be, the sooner I'd be able to make some mother-friends. I was extremely resistant to this fact until I had enough of the older kind of conversation on-site in Austin to sustain me. Miriam, sadly, left Austin a year after I arrived, and Felicity had always lived in Minneapolis, so while they were new friends, they weren't local friends. Petra, then, was my best source of old-style intimate woman-talk in Austin. As I grew closer to her and began to consider her an in-town intimate, my desperation for face-to-face, one-on-one substantive conversation began to lessen. And then there were the intensely satisfying and interesting interviews with a wide range of mothers. Between Petra and the interviews, I was eventually able to have enough intense discussions that I could entertain the possibility of also building friendships based on something else.

With one of my current mother-friends, I've only ever seen her alone once—in a coffee shop for forty-five minutes. With another, I've never been alone with her at all, never without children or children and husbands. I consider Sharon a very good friend, though, as well as the mother of Joseph's best friend.

Initially, I didn't know how to build a friendship with a woman that wasn't based on intense one-on-one conversation. What else was there to do? What I came to see over time—too much time, in my view—was that the dailiness of our shared interactions and our parallel lives as mothers (lives that contained many more similarities than differences) were a kind of intimacy. I may have turned to others to talk out the complexities of how I felt about the miscarriage following an unexpected pregnancy

I had in the spring of 2001—Alice, Duncan, Petra, Celia, Miriam, my brother Justin, a nurse, a therapist, an ex-boyfriend turned good friend and his wife, my mother, my mother's pro-choice neighbor, my mother-in-law— but it was Sharon who hugged me first and took care of my children so Duncan could accompany me to the doctor. That was worth a lot of words.

SIX

Mother and Child

When I became a mother, part of me thought I had to undergo a radical personality overhaul. I had been ambitious, prone to cursing, ironic, and rebellious—often in a rather adolescent form. None of this struck me as mom material.

Moms, I thought, were people who were simultaneously perky and selfless. *Sure I'll head up the PTA book sale! I'd love to.* They were enthusiastic about service—anything to help their children. They were efficient and resourceful.

I had some organizational skills, but I didn't always like using them. I have pretty simple desires: I like to read, write, talk intensely, and walk around. One and two, I do alone; three and four, I like to do with others. I do care deeply about the larger world, and this concern had led me prior to motherhood to develop and use my organizational skills, but I wasn't sure how the PTA would stack up against my desire to combat the death penalty, domestic violence, racism in the penal system, and U.S. aggression overseas. When pressed for time, how would I manage the mom stuff? Could I be a respectable, responsible mother without doing any of it?

I was afraid that moms were grown-up cheerleaders, people who stood on the sidelines of life and applauded as their sons—and nowadays daughters—performed athletic feats. They drove a lot, did laundry, stuffed countless sandwiches into Baggies, and listened attentively as their husbands discussed problems at work. They made big meat loaves and invited all the neighborhood kids to partake. They had other moms over for coffee and served fresh coffeecake. Where would I even get the recipe? My mother had made a coffeecake once in the '70s, but I believed it had come from a box. I didn't think contemporary mothers used box mixes. They cooked from scratch or else just got everything as takeout.

Much of this image, I knew, was a bit outdated—certainly the meat loaf and coffeecake were. Unfortunately many of the maternal expectations I saw as more modern struck me as equally frightening and possibly more arduous. While no one I knew thought women should smile while "running the new electric waxer over the spotless kitchen floor" as Betty Friedan so aptly described a key expectation for middle-class mothers of the 1950s and early '60s, now you simply had to raise a perfect child.* Contemporary married mothers were still supposed to care for their husbands and homes—I never saw a house as consistently messy and chaotic as mine—but the real focus, the real pressure, surrounded the child.

---

* Betty Friedan, *The Feminine Mystique* (New York: Dell Publishing, 1983), p. 18. Originally published by W.W. Norton in 1963.

At least in Austin, attachment parenting was the child-rearing system with the most cachet in the late '90s and early new millennium. It was touted as both ancient and modern, a combination I initially found perplexing. It was ancient, sometimes even called timeless, because unspecified groups of native women in Africa and Asia had apparently practiced it successfully for eons. On the other hand, it was modern because it solidly rejected American postwar admonitions to feed and put baby to sleep on a strict schedule. While the thwarted, bored, and depressed women Betty Friedan so eerily depicted in *The Feminine Mystique* had to do mind-numbing tasks for the sake of house, man, and child all day long, at least they knew with certainty when baby's naptime was. Attachment parenting, if practiced fully, required that you carry your baby with you all day in a sling, nurse on demand all day and all night, let baby doze on her own schedule during the day (in your arms), and let her sleep in the bed with you all night long.*

Perhaps it had been harsh, even cruel, to let a hungry baby scream for fifty minutes if four hours hadn't passed since her last feeding. On the other hand, based on the exhausted faces and bodies I saw around me—at La Leche League meetings, in the midwife's office, at library sing-alongs—full adherence to attachment parenting could nearly kill a woman. Certainly, I feared, it could kill a woman who wanted to be a writer, a woman who needed time alone.

---

* *The Baby Book* by William Sears, M.D., and Martha Sears, R.N. (Boston: Little, Brown, and Company, 2003). This is the most exhaustive explanation of attachment parenting. I read the original 1993 version, which has since been updated.

In addition to the prescriptions of attachment parenting, I also felt a variety of yuppie pressures raging around me. Good new-millennial mothers played Mozart sonatas to their children beginning—but certainly not ending—in utero, showed them black-and-white flashcards within days of birth, learned and administered elaborate infant massage techniques, trotted their children to a panoply of stimulating activities, and gained a veritable Ph.D. in child development through independent research and reading, though not for actual degree credit.

Not that I would ever advocate a return to the disheartening days Friedan described so well in *The Feminine Mystique*, but I wondered if popping a few Valium and vacuuming the hell out of your house wouldn't actually be easier than what seemed to be asked of contemporary mothers. At least children in the '50s, '60s, and '70s—and I was one who unquestionably benefited from this—got a bit of breathing room and free play. With attachment parenting requirements, yuppie pressures, and fear of neighborhood crime, a child in the new millennium might not get a free moment alone in which to develop her own imagination. Neither would her mother.

I made myself unhappy—though I had a lot of help from books and various experts around me—because I thought, at least in my most anxious moments, that I had to become someone else as a mother, someone cheerful, selfless, and aggressively devoted to my children's enrichment.

I didn't want to do this! I certainly hadn't been trained in school in the equality-minded '70s and '80s to step eagerly into the background, and then fill my life by caring for, and pushing, my children from there. I had my paella fantasy—and I clung to it like a talisman—but I also had a contradictory image of a martyred but directive woman who worked behind the scenes while her husband and children lived their lives on front stage.

I knew what a stereotype was, even one that was coming from a mishmash of sources. I knew what social pressure was. I even knew what hegemony was. None of this knowledge stopped me from thinking I had to become, at least partially, someone else as a mother.

To a large extent, my children stopped me. "What do *you* want to do, Mommy?" they would ask, and I didn't get the feeling they wanted me to lie. They wanted me to witness them in their worlds, to see them engaged in what they liked doing, but they also wanted us to figure out things we enjoyed together. I also think, though I have less direct evidence for this, that Ben and Joseph wanted me to figure out what I needed to do by myself in order to be happy, and to do it. How much good, really, was time spent with a depressed and weeping mother? Sure, they have begged me, on occasion, to take them to the mall to buy Pokémon cards, an activity they know I don't relish. But much more often, my sons are eager to find something that we all like doing. They're not satisfied for me to act like a hyper stress-bunny or a selfless automaton. "Hello, is anyone home?" they'll say, knocking on my head, if I seem to be slipping away.

Dorothy Parker wrote these words about marriage, but they strike me as applying equally well to the mother-child relationship: "Two people cannot go on and on and on, doing the same things year after year, when only one of them likes doing them . . . and still be happy."* Along similar lines, the principal at Joseph's elementary school once told me proudly about the magnet on her refrigerator: "If Momma ain't happy, ain't *nobody* happy."

With the help of my children, I gradually stopped trying to morph into some jumble of old and new maternal stereotypes and prescriptions. It took me so long—three and a half years of rather frenzied Gymboree-like activities—because the cultural pressure was still coming at me, from all directions as far as I could tell. And it was confusing. I couldn't figure out what, exactly, to refute. I couldn't figure out what a truly alternative mother-persona would look like. I'd always thought hippies were countercultural, yet the 1990s self-identified hippies I knew advocated attachment parenting—or AP—more adamantly than any other group in town. It seemed so hard on women. And making life hard for women has always struck me as traditional rather than alternative. In terms of what an actual woman's daily life would be like, I didn't see how AP would lead to anything more liberating than what conservative Christians, for example, might advise. At least conservatives occasionally used bottles.

What *should* I do as a mother? Nothing, other than kissing, struck me as obvious. I watched other mothers, read how-to books, and relied on stereotypes in part because I was ignorant. Especially when my children were very young, I was never quite sure what to do with them. Duncan and I figured most things out by trial and

---

* Dorothy Parker, "The Banquet of Crow," *Complete Stories* (New York: Penguin, 2003). Originally published in *The New Yorker*.

error. Still, there was considerable room for anxiety and doubt.

When Joseph was an infant, he had bright, wide eyes that seemed eager to take in everything. He reminded me of myself at my most curious and open to the world, my least depressed. Whenever he cried, I figured he was bored. In retrospect, I think he might have been tired—he wasn't much of a sleeper. But I'd carry him around the house in a front pack for what seemed like hours on end, circling by the objects that appeared to be his favorites, and making commentary: *There's the pink vase Grandpa gave me. See how the light shines through it? Here we are at the washing machine. Touch it with your toe. Woo, it's cold! There's Mommy's poster of the crazy ladies. They don't look crazy to me, they look sad.*

When I was too tired to carry Joseph around in the Baby Björn and we'd already exhausted all the outdoor options, sometimes I'd roll around the house on Duncan's blue office chair, Joseph sitting squatly on my lap. As long as we were moving—and I was talking—he was happy. When I stopped, he'd often cry unless he was breast-feeding or sleeping. Despite the frequent—if not lengthy—activities of food and rest, there was still a lot of time to kill, and I was never really sure what to do, other than talk and make observations.

Ben was more easily entertained. He didn't have to be constantly moving. He could sit contentedly beside me with some toys while I loaded the dishwasher. As he got older, he'd stuff the toys in the dishwasher as well as try to pull the sharpest knives out for play, but it was all very good natured and since I was right there, easily headed off before calamity struck. As soon as Ben could walk, he'd toddle behind me as I raced around trying—unsuccessfully, on the whole—to bring order to the chaos and clutter in our house. Ben would watch me carefully and then offer his own version of help: hairbrush off the floor and into the toilet, potted plant off the desk and upside down in the trash, spare change out of the cup and into the VCR. Certainly it was frustrating—Ben broke the VCR and the cassette player in the car by stuffing quarters in—but it was impossible to be really mad since he was so cute, so earnest, and so clearly following me. My own frantic and repetitive straightening hardly seemed any more sensible than his did.

During my period of hermithood, the time when I was struggling hardest with domestic life and feeling most confused and guilty about my unhappiness, my mother once offered this insight: "Ben will be talking soon, darling. Remember how much better you felt when Joseph could talk? You didn't really hit your stride as a mother until then."

I was a bit offended. Had I really been a hideous incompetent throughout Joseph's preverbal babyhood? Was I failing now with Ben? Certainly, I feared I was. Some days I couldn't leave the house other than to teach my classes, and I was weeping fairly often. My hormones were fine, and even Louise didn't think I needed antidepressants. Could my problem be as simple as wanting my baby to talk?

Even a few words from my children were so welcome, such riches of communication. When we went camping overnight with another family when Ben was fourteen months old, he began crying adamantly at bedtime, pointing to the tall pines blowing in the wind, shaking his head, and saying, "No, no, no!" I felt I knew exactly what he meant. Actually, I meant it as well, and I would have said it, in my own words, if I hadn't been embarrassed because we were with new friends and camping is supposed to be fun, or protective of Duncan who was worried about me and hopeful that the outdoors would make me feel better.

Here was my interpretation of Ben's words, or word: *People aren't supposed to sleep outside, under trees. I don't want to sleep in a tent with those big waving things over my head. Where's my bed? I want to go home.*

Well said, little man, I thought to myself. A few months later when the friends generously asked us to go camping again, Duncan and Joseph happily camped while Ben and I went along for part of the day, then drove home to sleep comfortably in our own beds.

Was my mother right that my sadness would lift when Ben could talk? Interestingly enough, my return to emotional health did correspond rather directly with Ben's increasing vocabulary, but of course I don't think this explains everything. If it did, I would have written a different—and shorter—book. Still, I had to acknowledge that my mother had a point.

When my sons could talk, there was a voice—other than my own—to help me combat the silliest and most mother-abnegating cultural prescriptions. I needed help. When it was just me against the culture, I felt distinctly that I was losing, on occasion. And my fellow soldiers couldn't be just anyone. Duncan tried valiantly to help, and he was incredibly astute about social pressures, but he wasn't a mother. He also didn't have any more child-rearing experience than I did. While I would have loved to have a CR group of other new, and more experienced, mothers in the late '90s, no one could do the job of stopping my guilt better than Ben and Joseph. If they were okay, and they could verbalize this to me, then I didn't have to worry so much about the barrage of cultural mandates.

I did learn to read preverbal cues from my babies with a fair degree of accuracy. But as long as they couldn't talk, I was still periodically afraid that I was doing something terribly wrong. They were so small and fragile. What if I didn't buy the proper side-sleeper pillow, and I found them blue and lifeless one morning? I felt assaulted by alarmist information, which translated itself into a fairly constant stream of internal chatter: *Watch out! Your child might grow up to be a psychopath if you let him see cartoons. No refined sugar before two or his teeth will rot out! He'll be insecure if you wean him before he initiates the process! He needs fresh air, socialization, to be nestled close to your body all day long; he needs Mozart, he needs Bach, he needs a small mirror beside his changing table to help integrate his ego.*

Part of me knew that much of this was overblown, even ridiculous. Part of me also knew that the urgency of the directives I heard was wed to American consumerism as well as anxieties about women's independence and membership in the workforce. I could have written a great paper critiquing this kind of advertising and advice-wielding before I became a mother. As a mother, part of me fell subject to it.

When Joseph and Ben could talk, though, the advice-giving voices inside my head grew quieter. I could tell that my sons liked jokes instead of continual earnestness or aggressive stimulation because they laughed at the jokes. I could see that they didn't need to go to Gymboree, Kindermusik, swimming lessons, and violin because they said—clearly—that they wanted to stay home and play.

Also, I myself am a talker. When my sons could talk, I suddenly had pals, in addition to Duncan, living with me. This was a wonderful transformation.

Nothing makes me happier than engaged conversation with my children. When Ben was two and a half, he told me at breakfast: "Mommy, remember when you were in the water with all the animals? You were making your cheeks go a funny way, like this." He stopped to suck his cheeks in, then let them out, like a goldfish.

Joseph, who was vigorously stirring his Oatios around and around, grew interested. "Ben, when? When was that?"

Ben continued to explain. "And a cactus pushed me in the water."

Joseph and I looked at each other, puzzled. What was Ben talking about? Then Joseph's face suddenly lit up. "Ben, you had a dream!" he said with excitement.

"Yeah," Ben said, "I had a dream."

"Sweetie, do you know what a dream is?" I asked.

Joseph didn't wait for Ben to answer. "A dream is when you think something while you're asleep," he explained.

These are the parenting moments I love more than anything—fascinating, unexpected, verbal, and full of wonder. My mother was right. I do love the talking. And that has a lot to do with why I'm not much of a baby person. The long struggle through infancy was well worth the wait to be right here, hearing my son recount the first dream he could articulate.

When I felt like myself as a mother rather than someone trying to squeeze herself into a hodgepodge image of Perfect Mom, I did verbal things with my sons, beginning long before they could talk. I talked to them, read to them, and played the piano—or rather plunked out melodies with my right hand. I got songbooks and sang all the old camp songs I knew and loved.

I wasn't much good at playing in other ways. When Joseph was three, he burst into tears one day after trying unsuccessfully to get me to sit still with him. "Why won't you play trains with me like Daddy does?" he asked mournfully.

I felt terrible. He was sobbing, and it was unquestionably my fault. I couldn't stop racing around—cleaning something up, opening the mail, answering the phone. Sure, I was busy, but couldn't I manage to sit still with my child for a few minutes? I could sit still if we were reading, singing, or talking. Otherwise, I was, frankly, a bit impatient. There was so much to do—I couldn't, didn't want to, stop and roll a train on a track. How could I explain this to Joseph? More important, how could I soothe his feelings? I decided to try to talk my way out, like I always do when I'm in trouble.

After I'd hugged him awhile and apologized for promising to play and then repeatedly getting up, I said, "When I was a little girl, girls and boys didn't play with the same things at all. It was weird, really. Girls played with dolls. I've never actually played with trains. I don't know how, and I don't yet see what the point is. You'll have to teach me, okay?"

This led to an intensive train-play tutorial, which turned out to be just great, from my perspective. I got to listen intently to Joseph talk, to notice how he structured his sentences, how he walked in circles and gestured wildly with his hands while explaining. He seemed to enjoy teaching me, too, although arguably not as much as he would have a gung ho train playmate.

Perhaps this is the rationalization of a tired person, but I feel I'm doing some of the best parenting I'm capable of when I lie on the floor and chat with my kids as they play. I watch for a while, let them explain things to me if they want to, then maybe ask a question: Do the giraffes always sleep in the hotel, or is that just for special occasions? Or else I verbally notice things—the blue train feels smooth, this man's tummy smells like a new car.

Over time, it became clear in our house that Mommy talked and Daddy played. I was aware that this split fit nicely into traditional gender stereotypes. *Of course Daddy plays trains better than I do,* I later thought, defensively. *He can play quite happily because he's not worried about the clothes getting moldy in the washer. As far as I can tell, he hasn't given the laundry any thought at all—let alone touched it—in months.*

My inability to sit still and play couldn't be blamed entirely on Duncan, though. Part of my lack of playing was simply inclination. I could try to fake it, but basically I was interested in and engaged, primarily, by talk. Otherwise, I felt like I'd rather race around and complete a task. Duncan, on the other hand, truly enjoyed play.

About a year after Joseph's sad question about my

playing abilities, I heard a rustling in the upstairs room where the boys had built an elaborate train track with Duncan's help earlier in the day. It was nearly midnight now. Were we infested by rats or squirrels? I tiptoed in, and there was Duncan, building a new track. He looked really embarrassed to see me. "Busted," I said and smiled. At that moment, I loved the kind of father he was. I certainly didn't have the desire or patience to create a new train route in the middle of the night.

Fortunately for me, Ben and Joseph seem to enjoy straight-up talk almost as much as play. One morning at 5:40, I was woken by four-year-old Joseph bouncing on our bed. "Let's play a game, Mommy!"

"Couldn't we just talk?" I grumbled.

"All right-y," he said. "But it has to be about something *exciting.*"

"Like what?" I whispered hoarsely, eyes still closed.

Joseph appeared to think intently for a few seconds while continuing to bounce. Then all of a sudden, he shouted with exuberance, "I know—Siamese twins!"

This is my child, a chip off the old maternal block. Joseph is relentlessly curious, especially about the odder aspects of human nature, and he has an ear for controversy. Whenever he hears Duncan and me talking in low yet animated tones, his ears stand up. "What? Mom, what?" he asks many times a day.

The morning he offered up Siamese twins as exciting discussion matter, I got a clear image of myself at seven, pigtailed, in a navy blue sailor dress, sprawled out on the gray plush backseat of my grandmother's Cadillac, ears wide open, as my mother and grandmother talked up front. Smoke from their parallel cigarettes filled the car, as did the smell of my grandmother's Bellodgia perfume. "Who's dying?" I'd ask eagerly. "Whose husband isn't right in the head? What happened to Ethel's leg? Where did Shelton run off to and when's he coming back? Who put Vernon in the institution? What's a crying shame?" I listened to every word my mother and grandmother exchanged and begged for clarification of anything remotely juicy.

I didn't always get the detailed answers I was hoping for, but I was in information-seeking for the long haul. Joseph and Ben seem headed the same way.

We first came on the subject of Siamese twins when Joseph was complaining about Ben following him around the house. "If you guys were Siamese twins, you'd have to be together all the time," I think I might have said. This led to about a billion questions from both of them, and we eventually ended up at the library checking out all the kids' books on Siamese twins (there were three).

Earlier, Joseph had been fascinated by the *Titanic.* Ben took up the disastrous ship as well, a few years later. They both spent hours poring over the catalog from the *Titanic* exhibit, which my friend Miriam brought with her once when she came to visit. She generously left it behind when it was clear that the boys couldn't bear to give it up. We all tried to imagine different escape plans, possible ways to avoid freezing. "I'd get drunk and coat myself in vegetable oil," Duncan offered. We talked about why women and children are supposed to get in lifeboats first, how we might come back and save Daddy. Why were the poor people locked below? What makes rich people rich? What would it be like to live on an iceberg forever?

These were not cheerful discussions. They did seem valuable, though, and they were engaging—for all of us. Yet sometimes I worry. Is it wrong to talk at length about mass drowning and birth defects with young children? Duncan and I have also talked intensely to Ben and Joseph about deforestation, slavery, and the death penalty, taking the kids with us to the governor's mansion to protest executions. Once they put on white gloves, like us, and shouted: "No blood on our hands!"

I feel fairly confident about our rally attendance, but I also suspect that I've personally erred on the side of overemphasizing the horrific at least a few times. I worry about the times when I've emphasized the horrific just for interest's sake, rather than as something that needs to be explained and then worked against, from my perspective—like the death penalty or American imperialism. I haven't sought out longitudinal studies on the effect of morbid subjects on children, though, and my sons aren't old enough yet for me to know if there's been irreparable damage from some of our family discussion matter.

It's terrifying to be a mother, to never know for sure if what you're doing could, or will, harm your child. I could walk on eggshells literally all the time. Many hours, I have. Other times, I've tried to let loose and be who I actually am—someone keenly interested in the bizarre, the unusual, and struggles for social justice. From what I can tell, my children seem to like this better. We'll see how it turns out in the long run.

Let me be clear, though, about our daily life: We don't

do elaborate research at the library or attend political protests all the time. Sometimes Ben and Joseph watch TV while I lie on the floor and try to read, or else clean the kitchen in a half-assed manner. Sometimes I yell at them. Sometimes I cry. Sometimes we eat at McDonald's. Sometimes they play together while I listen, forlornly, to Jimi Hendrix. *There must be some kind of way out of here Said the joker to the thief. There's too much confusion, I can't get no relief.*

Occasionally, we do more than talk about bizarre phenomena. When Petra told me about a feminist performance artist from Paris who was coming to talk about the unnecessary surgery she'd had as a protest against the objectification of women's bodies, I was intrigued. Apparently, the artist had recently had horns implanted in her forehead.

"That sounds totally screwed up," I said. "When is it?"

"Thursday at four."

"I'll be there."

The artist's talk was scheduled to begin thirty minutes before Duncan's class let out around the corner. I couldn't think of a baby-sitter who'd be free at that time, but more important, I wanted to take the boys along. I pretty much use all of their time with baby-sitters doing things I absolutely cannot do with them—writing and teaching. Other times, I like to take them with me as much as possible, to show them pieces of the adult world, provided they occur before bedtime. We'd just returned from a vacation in France, and it would be good, I thought, for the boys to hear thirty minutes of French. I was also itching to do something irreverent and interesting, something edgy. I wanted my sons to do it with me.

Of course, I had some doubts. Ben was just three, and the lecture was sure to be dense, odd, and solely in French, though there would be a translator. *We'll just sit in the back*, I thought, *so we can make a speedy exit if we need to leave before Duncan gets there.*

"Guys," I said on Tuesday as Ben and Joseph ate after-school pretzels and Go-gurts, "I just heard about a lady who has horns."

"What? What are you talking about, Mom?" Joseph asked excitedly.

"Is the lady a goat?" Ben added.

"No, she's not a goat. She has horns, though. She had them implanted in her head."

"Why?" Joseph asked. "Why would someone do that?"

"That's what I want to find out. Do you guys want to come along?"

"Yeah!" they both shouted.

Thursday afternoon, we drove by the park on our way to the lecture. I saw the moms pushing the same swings back and forth, back and forth. I was a bit nervous about our outing, but I was so glad we weren't going to the park instead.

A fellow mother did call, just as we were leaving, to ask us to join her and her kids at the park. "I'm sorry, we're just heading out to a program at UT," I said.

"What is it? A puppet show?" she asked good-naturedly. "We saw the Muppets there last year, and it was really good."

"No, it's not a puppet show," I said. "To tell you the truth, it's not really for kids at all. It's in French, though, and I thought Ben and Joseph would enjoy that. Have fun at the park," I continued, "thanks for calling." I hung up, and we were free.

When we got to the studio, part of the Radio, Television, and Film School, it was packed. Petra had told me to come forty-five minutes early, but I knew the kids would never last forty-five minutes of waiting, then thirty minutes of dense French philosophy, even if it was delivered by someone with a very interesting head. We arrived fifteen minutes early, and there was no standing room at all, and there were absolutely no seats in the back. Thankfully, Petra had saved us two seats right in the middle of the studio. There'd be no way to make a discreet exit from those seats, however. I hoped for the best and put Ben on my lap and Joseph beside me. Petra introduced us to Nadia, her dissertation adviser, who was seated on Petra's other side. Nadia was wearing extremely hot leather pants.

The artist began to speak and to show slides of the work she'd done prior to having her surgeries. The boys were happy, at first, just to hear French. Joseph even recognized a few words and tapped my wrist excitedly when he heard *la table, rouge, la fille*. And they were both fascinated by the horns—tiny stubs in her temples—as well as her Cruella de Ville hairstyle. Ben was quite taken with the slide projector as well. They sat happily and quietly for twenty minutes or so of the talk.

Then Ben began to fidget and ask for a snack, which I did have but had to find in the plastic bag stuffed under our chair. "Shhhh!" Nadia shushed us.

I felt pretty bad right then. My intention had certainly

not been to disturb other audience members, to impede their ability to hear. I didn't want to be an inconsiderate citizen! If only there'd been room at the back. I always sat in the back when I took my children to adult events. I couldn't always hear everything, but it seemed like the best compromise solution for everyone involved. Should I have turned away when there were no seats in the back? Should we push our way through the crowd now and get out, or could Ben hold on a bit longer?

Five minutes later, it became clear that the artist was going to show actual video footage of her most recent operation—the implantation of the horns. *Oh, shit,* I thought and then, *Please hurry, Duncan!* There was no need to panic, I told myself. If the lights went down, we would simply climb over everyone and get out. My children were not going to see open-face surgery—that was taking our outing too far. I didn't personally want to miss the video, but of course I would take Ben and Joseph out if necessary.

The situation was truly nerve wracking, but I also couldn't help but note that I was extremely happy. I had Ben on my lap, I was holding Joseph's hand, my good friend was by my side, and a woman with full-fledged horns was in front of us, speaking a gorgeous Parisian French. I felt like myself, my whole self, in public, and this was incredibly—and sadly—rare. Here I was, a mother and a person who enjoyed unusual events at a quirky, arguably feminist, and above all, interesting program with my children. What a way to spend the afternoon!

Duncan arrived in the nick of time, and I was able to squeeze the kids through the crowd without too much disruption. "Thanks so much for coming with me, boys," I whispered at the doorway, and they responded by doing the shashy-mooshy dance in the hall, one of their signals of excitement. They were excited, I thought, to have come with me to something out of the ordinary, and also to now be leaving with Daddy.

The next morning, we talked at breakfast about why someone might choose to have unnecessary surgery since this was the question that had most interested all three of us. Ben had quite sensibly asked on our way to the lecture, "Why doesn't she just wear paper horns? Then she could take them off if she ever wanted to."

I told the boys that I'd seen the video of her surgery— or rather parts of it, since I'd had to turn my face away most of the time, it was so unsettling. "One man fainted," I said, "he had to be carried out into the hall." Ben and Joseph were as excited by this fact as I had been.

As to why she did it, I said I still couldn't figure it out even after watching the surgery and hearing another full hour of explanation. I said I thought she was interested in what happens when a body is cut, in experiencing that for herself, but Petra and I had also wondered whether she might want people to keep looking at her. In the earlier nude works she'd shown us from her twenties, her body and face had been unlined and conventionally beautiful. Now that she's older, I told the boys, she might think she has to work harder to get people to keep looking at her.

"That sounds like the queen in Snow White," Joseph said.

Everything about this conversation and the prior day's outing interested me. Actually, the French artist's speech

236 * Faulkner Fox

itself had been a bit dry. But I loved talking about the issues her surgery raised with Petra in a skanky bar across the street after the show, and I loved my sons' questions and insights. Before I had children, I suspected that one quality I possessed might make me quite well-suited for motherhood: a love of "why" questions. Children ask "why" all the time, veteran parents had warned, and I couldn't wait. *That's what I do, too,* I thought but didn't always admit since it struck me as a somewhat impractical modus operandi for an adult woman.

Part of the reason I'd been so unhappy in 1998–1999, the year of my hermithood, was because I'd partially lost the ability to ask "why." I'd been so caught up in maternal cultural dictates and my own reactive judgmentalism—as well as being incredibly busy with a toddler and a baby—that I couldn't do what is most fundamental to who I am: go around investigating why people do and think what they do.

As predicted by veteran parents, Ben and Joseph both asked "why" as soon as they could string a question together. My sons are often the most curious people I encounter in a given day. When we go out into the world together—and even an errand can turn into an adventure—we're like three Sherlock Holmeses on the loose. Not always, of course. Sometimes I'm irritable and rushed, and I just want to whip around and cross as many things off my list as possible. Other times, I'm so thankful to have my sons with me. I hate errands, and while I have to move more slowly with my children along, the world is a lot more interesting that way.

As soon as my sons could talk, it wasn't just me alone

during weekday afternoons against a barrage of cultural pressure and surrounded by moms who didn't seem nearly as interested in dissecting the meaning and source of the pressure as I was. Instead, I was part of a society of investigators. Two of us were quite small, but our avidity and curiosity were large.

Lots of less-than-fully-employed mothers, I realized, view themselves this way—as members of a weekday society with their children. Dad, if he's part of the household, is typically at work. Meanwhile, the mother and children form a harbor against whatever she perceives as dangerous and wrong in the larger world. For the hippie moms I knew, they and their children faced off against processed food, regimentation in public schools, long-houred jobs, and the competitive, sped-up pace of mainstream culture. For conservative Christian mothers, the adversaries looked more like a secular public school curriculum with explicit sex education, lasciviousness on TV, and lack of respect for elders among children other than their own. While I knew the isolation of mother and children, the harbor-against-the cruel-world model itself, was part of what had been causing me distress all along, I also retreated to it, on occasion. Ben and Joseph were curious, and they asked "why." I appreciated this enormously in a person, and I felt more like myself when I was around such people.

At times, then, I viewed our own nuclear trio as facing off against apathy, excessive TV and computer games, and unquestioning acceptance of the status quo. I could be as smug and self-righteous about these choices and values as any other mother I knew. I tried to emphasize the investigative impulse rather than the certainty that I was right about what activities we should pursue and avoid, but sometimes I slipped into know-it-all-ness.

At a Wiccan, or modern-day witchcraft, celebration of Brigit, the February 2 holiday that focuses on looking ahead to the work you plan to do in the upcoming spring, Duncan and I once watched a young woman vigorously toss a piece of paper into a bonfire then shout, "And I will know—from now on—that I am never, ever wrong!"

The ritual took place in the yard beside one of Austin's fringe theaters. When Duncan and I had arrived, we'd been instructed to write down on scraps of paper whatever we wanted to leave behind with the passing winter. Fear, anxiety, and stress had been offered up as examples. Later, each of us threw our paper into the fire in turn. I don't remember what I wrote. What I remember is the young woman's earnest and intent face and her vehement tone. She must have felt that people were trying to strip her of her sense of right and wrong, and, reasonably enough, she wanted to shore up her own self-confidence. Nevertheless, that young woman came to represent for me—fairly or unfairly—a certain self-righteousness that I found prevalent and disturbing in Austin's rich counter-culture.

I didn't want to engage in constant neurotic self-doubting, but I also didn't want to be too certain that I always, or even often, knew what was right for myself or my children. At our best, I felt that Ben, Joseph, and I kept open minds. Often this meant simply exploring our mutual interest areas, grotesque as some of them were: leeches, Siamese twins, earthquakes, shipwrecks, the possibility of life on other planets, unnecessary surgery, wizardry, and balloon travel. Occasionally our topics cut closer to home.

When I got pregnant in the spring of 2001, Ben, in particular, had lots of questions. While he isn't as driven toward the controversial, per se, as Joseph and I are, he's keenly interested in the cosmic, the extrasensory, the mechanical, and issues of life and death.

How did the baby get in there, Ben wanted to know. Had he and Joseph been in the same place? Had they been there at the same time, playing? What had they been wearing?

I answered Ben's questions with as much detail as he seemed to want. When he asked what the baby looked like right then, I took out *A Child Is Born* so I could show him a picture of an embryo at six weeks. As I turned to the right page, my heart sank because I knew the page well. It features a grotesque cystlike formation. When I'd been pregnant with Joseph and poring over the book nearly every day, I'd had to turn my face away and flip quickly past the six-week photo, it made me that queasy.

Ben seemed unfazed, and he studied the picture closely. "So basically," he said, "the baby looks really bad."

I laughed at his signature matter-of-factness and kissed his sweet head. Then we flipped forward to see how the baby would change, how it wouldn't always look so bad.

In real life, it didn't change enough. By ten weeks, the embryo was undersized, and its heartbeat had stopped. Duncan told the boys.

"What's that tiny sound?" Ben said the next morning as he lay in bed with us. "I hear the baby's heartbeat."

"I know you wish you did," I said. "I do too." And I did. I was devastated to be losing this child I hadn't planned or initially been sure I wanted at all.

The day after my miscarriage, Duncan went to work (though he was home by early afternoon to check on me), and Joseph went to kindergarten. Ben stayed home from preschool to keep me company. We didn't talk about the miscarriage. Instead, we went out in the yard and listened to the birds. We lay on the floor and did a Noah's Ark puzzle, then I sang the Noah's Ark song I'd learned at camp. We ate a nice lunch together—macaroni and cheese, one of our favorites.

The next day, when everyone was supposed to carry on as normal, I was really low. At breakfast when I couldn't stop crying, Duncan asked the boys if they knew what was wrong.

"MISCARRIAGE!" Ben shouted out proudly, as if he'd just answered "Atlanta, Georgia" correctly on a quiz show. His exuberant tone made us all laugh, even me.

That night when the boys were going to bed, Ben said, "Mommy, I don't want you to have another miscarriage. Try not to."

"Well, it's not really about trying," I said. "You can't always have a baby. Sometimes the baby doesn't live."

"Did you try really hard this time?" Joseph asked.

"No. Actually, I didn't try at all," I admitted.

"How did the baby get in there?" Joseph followed up.

I gave a brief description of sperm meeting egg, one significantly less elaborate than I'd given on prior occasions. Amazingly, there were no follow-up questions.

I turned out the light and sat between them on

Joseph's bed. "I tried really hard to have you guys," I said. "I've never wanted anything more than I wanted you two boys to be born. And here you are." I hugged Ben tightly to my chest, then did the same with Joseph.

While Duncan and I did tell the boys about my pregnancy fairly soon—certainly sooner than the twelve weeks many parents wait in order to minimize the risk of miscarriage before sharing the news with young children—we didn't tell them everything. We didn't tell them that we had seriously considered abortion upon finding out that I was pregnant. I couldn't think of a way how, a way to say I might not want someone who had started as they had. It was a lot easier to tell them two years later— as I did before the guests arrived at the thirtieth anniversary celebration of *Roe v. Wade* I was hosting—that women in general shouldn't be forced to have babies they didn't want or couldn't take care of.

The personal decision Duncan and I made about our own unplanned pregnancy was difficult, and I was certainly glad we'd had a choice to make. It also felt like an adult decision, not one I wanted to share with my three- and six-year-old sons.

✳✳✳

If the two extremes of possible maternal disclosure are reticence and fakery on the one side and brutal, age-inappropriate honesty on the other, I've decided to risk erring on the side of honesty. As I see it, either extreme can potentially harm a child. While trying not to go overboard, I've chosen to orient my mothering toward the end of the spectrum that does the least harm to me, fits best with my natural proclivities, and models behavior that I believe to be more authentic for my sons. It's also the end that leads to more intriguing talks and outings.

At his end-of-the-year first-grade picnic, Joseph whispered in my ear to ask if he could tell his teacher's aide that my cousin had been shot the prior month. Mercifully, my cousin Thomas, who'd had a harrowing scuffle with an unbalanced ex-roommate, was just fine, with only flesh wounds. Duncan had chastised me for letting Joseph know about the incident, though. "You try to keep it from him," I'd said. "He knew I had something juicy, and he wouldn't let up until he found out what it was." Still, I suspected Duncan was right.

At the first-grade picnic, I whispered back that Joseph could tell Miss Beth about Thomas's gunshot wounds, if he really wanted to. Suddenly shy, Joseph whispered back to me, "You tell her."

Miss Beth was staring at us by this point, waiting expectantly for whatever we had to say. She knew we were whispering about her. I took a small bite of my Sno-Kone, chewed it, then said, "Joseph wants you to know that my cousin was shot. He's completely fine now, but it was very scary."

"Oh, my goodness, that's terrible!" Miss Beth exclaimed. "I'm so glad he's all right." Then she looked at Joseph and smiled. "You, sir," she said, wagging her finger, "are quite the collector and dispenser of important news. We're really going to miss you in the first grade."

Joseph beamed then took a big bite of his own Sno-Kone through lips already dyed bright blue.

I'm fairly ashamed of this picnic exchange. Joseph and

I need to rein ourselves in a bit more concerning the spread of controversial information. I'm the mother—I should set a better example.

At my best moments with my sons, I haven't merely abetted them in spreading salacious facts for the sheer thrill of it. Instead, I've taken what I view as the cream of my education and natural proclivity (inquisitiveness) and left the rest (social anxiety, acute competitiveness, judgmentalism, love of gossip, and fear of failure) behind. Ben, Joseph, and I have simply gone around being curious together. I've loved this.

I haven't been satisfied, though, to investigate with my sons all day, every day. Part of me still wishes I had been, believes I would be a better mother that way. Sometimes I've wished that my desire to write could have submerged itself for a few years: *Good-bye, self. Hello, mother-person.* If anything, though, my desire to write grew stronger when I had children.

Writers need to be alone to write. They need to look keenly at the world—and they can have eager company, at least part of the time, while they look—but then they have to shut the world and other people out while they process and shape what they've seen into words.

Although Ben, Joseph, and I sometimes write children's stories together, adult writing isn't something we can work on jointly. I often miss my sons while I write, and sometimes I feel guilty as well. The guilt has been reflected back to me, amplified by the world, on countless occasions. As just one example, an editor who looked at an early draft of a chapter of this book rejected the manuscript with this comment: "If she's going to be home this much, she should be taking care of her children instead of writing about them."

What the editor said is, of course, what I myself think in my darkest, most guilty moments. God forbid that a woman could actually write *and* take care of her children. Or that children could amazingly enough survive, thrive no less, being cared for sizable chunks of the day by their father (remember him?) or loving and skilled baby-sitters and teachers.

I'm not nearly so guilty about working as a teacher, nor do I get as many guilt-provoking comments on that aspect of my life. While not everyone approves, more people are comfortable with a mother of young children working at a job than writing for uncertain pay. A job is viewed as less—or not at all—optional, and typically reads as less selfish than writing. That is unless the writing is akin to amateur knitting—something a mother fits into whatever tiny snippets of spare time she has. I've been too ambitious to write like that.

To a certain extent, every time I sit down to write, I have to quell anxiety. I've come to view it as simply part of the job. One of my most frequent anxieties centers on being away from my children while I write.

Before motherhood, I didn't know what tragedy would be worst in my life. Cancer? Rape? An onset of schizophrenia? The list of possible horrors was diverse and long. As a mother, I have absolute clarity: Losing one of my children is, by far, the worst thing that could happen. I'm so terrified of this that sometimes I bargain with God. Usually, I imagine a benevolent and peace-promoting deity. But when I come to God begging for my children's health and safety, I face a wrathful Old Testament God, whom I offer frantic and all-encompassing deals: *I'll never write again, I'll never sing, I'll never make love, never consume more than bread, water, and vitamins—just please don't take my child.*

I have the feeling sometimes that not being a full-time stay-at-home mother during my children's preschool years when we could have managed it financially is akin to taking my children for granted. And God doesn't like that—not the stern God I face at my most desperate. He punishes people who overlook what they have. At my most extreme, I could be a poster-child for the Christian right. *Beware, beware! Get back to the house, you selfish working woman, before terrible things happen.*

I could never actually be a conservative poster-child, of course. For one thing, I won't evangelize; I won't spread the guilt I sometimes feel to other women. I keep my fire and brimstone under wraps—it's solely directed at me.

One night as I was putting Joseph to bed, he said, "Mom, please go away. I have to say my prayer."

"I didn't know you said a prayer," I responded.

"Go away," he repeated.

"I'm going."

As I got to the door, he called out, "Mom, I always say the same thing." I turned to listen, as he so clearly wanted me to do.

"God, I'm going to bed," he said. "God, I have a good life. God, I have a good house."

I smiled widely. "What a wonderful prayer," I said. *And how different from my own desperate let's-make-a-deal supplications,* I thought. And then I made a note to myself:

Don't send Ben and Joseph to any Sunday school where they could get a harsh, wrathful image of God. Not that I went to such a church myself. I was brought up Episcopalian, a fairly restrained and stodgy faith. Still, I had a vivid imagination, and I hung on to the stories that horrified and perplexed me. How could God make Abraham offer up his son's life even if he did stop the death toll at the last minute? *I won't give up my sons, God. Pick something else. Name your price, and I'll do it.*

But he's never given me a price. There is no bargain I can strike—with anyone or anything—to keep my children safe. This fact is much harder to accept than any self-deprivation I can dream up. Denying myself—of a career, a sex life, good nutrition, sleep—is no guarantee of anything for my sons, other than a less-than-happy mother.

I've never loved anyone like I love Ben and Joseph, and the intensity of this love can make my thinking foggy, desperate, conservative, and superstitious. It's why even the craziest cultural mandates can still affect me, on occasion.

✳✳✳

While I've had some guilt about writing at all, I've had additional guilt about writing this book in particular. When my cousin Ian and his girlfriend dropped by a few months ago, Joseph told them about my book. "My mom's writing a book about stress and motherhood," he said. "She's *really* stressed out."

Yikes. I didn't want Joseph to think this. What if he thought he'd personally caused my stress? He had, on occasion, but I didn't want him to know it. Two years prior when I'd told an old high school friend what I was doing, her immediate response had been, "Wow, your kids are really gonna need therapy in about twenty years."

Indeed, that's the fear. What a mother does, says—and in my case—writes, could cause deep harm to her children. And yet we all go on every day, doing what we believe is necessary. In my case, I feel it's my responsibility as a writer, a feminist, and a mother to call a spade a spade, as I see it. I've been afraid to write this book, but I've done it anyway because it appears to me that a lot of women are suffering—facing hard circumstances and challenges, then guilt-tripping themselves about whatever path they take. If I could possibly do something, write something, that might alleviate some of the guilt, then I had to try.

And yet I've worried about having a cover proclaiming the imperfection of my life lying around the house. What would Ben and Joseph think—that Mom didn't love them? That they'd made her unhappy? Maybe they'd think that perfection shouldn't really be the point of life, but that might be too much sophistication to expect from a five- and an eight-year-old. Certainly it's more sophistication than I myself can always grasp. Ben, Joseph, and I are all captivated, on occasion, by myths of heroic selves living in perfect lands.

✳✳✳

At ages four and five, Joseph was utterly entranced by King Arthur. Not that many years prior, I'd been quite taken with King Arthur's sister, Morgan Le Fay, and the world of witchcraft she was said to inhabit. When I met a contemporary Druid at my friend Melinda's Santa Fe wedding in the spring of 2000—the height of Joseph's King

Arthur phase—he and I began to talk excitedly about
Druids, witchcraft, and King Arthur. Cedric told me that
modern-day British Druids were the only people who had
access to Stonehenge anymore, due to vandalism and graf-
fiti. On the winter and summer solstices, Druids were
allowed to do the rituals they had successfully persuaded
the British government were their spiritual birthright on
the actual rocks of Stonehenge. Everyone else had to stand
a hundred yards away—on the solstices and on every
other day of the year.

I told Cedric, who also had a five-year-old son, that
Joseph pored over pictures of Stonehenge, convinced that
King Arthur's uncle was buried there. "Why don't you
join us for the solstice?" Cedric said, noting that the
Druids could accommodate several "companions," or
guests, at the ritual.

When I floated this idea by Duncan, he was excited.
He vividly remembered playing on the rocks of Stonehenge as a child, and he wanted Ben and Joseph to at least
have a chance to touch the ancient stones. If we had to
temporarily join a Druid ritual in order to do so, all the
more interesting. We already had plane tickets for a long-
anticipated June vacation in France, and we figured we
could take a boat over to Poole and make our way up to
Stonehenge for the solstice weekend. Joseph was ecstatic
about the idea, and Ben, at two-and-a-half, was quickly
caught up in Joseph's excitement.

There were three actual Druid rituals held on the solstice: midnight, dawn, and noon the following day. We
decided that I would attend the midnight and dawn
events while Duncan slept with the boys in a nearby

hotel, then we'd all participate at noon. Certainly I had the most claim to Druidism, tenuous as my link was. Cedric had explained that the Druids were the male counterparts to the witches in the days of Stonehenge, and I'd been investigating and learning from witches since my year in New Orleans. One of us had to stay up all night since people weren't allowed to just show up for the easiest noon ritual. I would do the nighttime rituals so we could all do the third.

This hardly constituted the kind of selflessness I'd been afraid of as a new mother. Sleeplessness would be involved, but everything else seemed a bit too odd—and interesting—to count as full-blown maternal sacrifice. On the other hand, my solo participation in the midnight and dawn rituals didn't strike me as particularly selfish, either. I loved unusual religious events and attended them often, sometimes by myself and sometimes with Duncan or the boys. But I wouldn't have made my way to Stonehenge for the summer solstice alone—certainly not when I was the mother of a five- and a two-year-old. It simply wasn't that high on my personal agenda. We were going to Stonehenge because of Joseph's interest as much as mine, as well as to relive a positive moment from Duncan's childhood.

Come to think of it, a Druid ritual at Stonehenge was just about the perfect vacation activity for our particular family. Duncan had lived in England for a year when he was a child, Joseph was enthralled by King Arthur and Merlin, I enjoyed unusual religious rituals, and Ben liked big rocks as well as building structures from blocks that looked a bit like miniature Stonehenges. No one was sacrificing or compromising for the sake of anyone else's agenda. This must be what people meant by family fun!

As a child, I'd gone with my family on a series of ski trips in the '70s and early '80s. After valiantly taking beginner ski lessons for several years, my mother decided she really didn't want to ski at all. Instead, she began to spend her vacation mornings sitting happily in the lodge at the bottom of the hill, reading and drinking hot chocolate, until the rest of us returned, flushed and hungry. We all had lunch together, then my mother returned to her book while the rest of us hit the slopes. This was my image of a mother asserting herself on vacation, and it was a fairly empowering one. My mother grew increasingly confident about opting out of whatever recreational events my father had planned.

I wouldn't say that a ski trip was something my parents fully co-authored, though. My mother hates the cold, and it struck her as counterintuitive to go somewhere colder than Virginia in February and call it a vacation, *the* family vacation, in fact.

What I most wanted as a mother, and what I most feared I couldn't have, was the ability to author my own life. Not as a lone ranger, per se—I'd willingly, if fearfully, given that up when I'd married Duncan—but as someone with a strong voice in what we did on a daily basis, at home as well as on vacation.

As I thought about our Stonehenge plans, they seemed rather extraordinary. I'd never heard of a family vacation where the mother did odd rituals all night long while the father cared for their young children. Not that this didn't happen, of course—I just didn't know of any such occurrences. Several of the Druid higher-ups—all bearded white men in their thirties and forties—had young children, I later found out. Rodney, the Druid leader, had a two-year-old. All of these children were being cared for by the Druid wives during the rituals.

When we got to Stonehenge the afternoon of the solstice, it was raining. We checked into the Hotel St. George, built circa 950—"King Arthur's time!" we told Joseph excitedly—and we were all asleep by 8 P.M.

At 11:30 P.M., I got up and drove the three miles to Stonehenge. In the car park, I gave the police my name and was allowed in. I found Cedric, and he introduced me to several other folks. There were about sixty of us—mostly British, but with a few Americans and Canadians mixed in.

After an hour-long meditation on a mound in a nearby field, we returned to the car park where a silver-haired woman took my measurements and issued me a nicely starched white robe. I asked her if she could just give me the robes for Ben, Joseph, and Duncan then. There was a considerable amount of searching in the back of the chartered Druid bus, and then the sad answer—there were no child-sized robes.

"Couldn't they just wear long white shirts?" I asked.

"Oh, no," was her reply. She called Rodney over, and he explained that the Druids were on a rather short leash with the British government, and their legitimacy could be questioned at any moment. The solstice rituals had to be extremely well-organized and circumspect in order to distinguish the Druids from the other random New Agers and hippies who had also come to Stonehenge en masse for the summer solstice. It simply wouldn't do to have young children in ad hoc attire participating in what needed to be a neat and orderly show.

I felt sorely disappointed, as well as a bit bamboozled. Cedric apologized profusely and tried to make me feel better by saying that his son had never participated and that the noon ritual went on for over two hours and wasn't really kid friendly. Still, I wanted Ben and Joseph to touch Stonehenge. I wanted Duncan to get to touch it again, as an adult. I wanted us all to be together on those magical rocks. We'd come such a long way. How would I break the news to Ben and Joseph? This wasn't shaping up to be the perfect family vacation activity after all. Here I was in a parking lot in the rain at 2 A.M. with a bunch of very interesting strangers. I figured I'd better make the best of it, as well as taking careful mental notes so I could tell Ben, Joseph, and Duncan about everything I'd seen and done. If I had to be their emissary, I wanted to be a thorough one.

At 3:10, we started lining up for the dawn ritual. We left the car park at 3:40, and the light was totally different every five minutes. Miraculously, it had temporarily stopped raining, and as Cedric had foretold, it was absolutely stunning to see the sun rise directly over the headstone of Stonehenge from our position inside the circle of stones. The stones had been precisely arranged—by the Druids, Cedric said—so that the sun would rise this way on the solstice. That's why so many people were camped out in the fields surrounding Stonehenge on June 21. I tried to memorize everything about the feel of the rocks and the look of the sun so I could tell all the details to Duncan and the boys.

I got back to the hotel in time for breakfast, and I broke the sad news about the lack of small robes, which Ben and Joseph took fairly well. "Kiss the stones for King Arthur and all his relatives and knights," Joseph directed me, and I promised that I would.

At 11:30 A.M., we all headed to Stonehenge. In the parking lot, I got back into my robe, which the boys loved. They kept fingering the soft folds of the pleats. "You look like a preacher, Mom!" Joseph said. Actually, I was a bit worried that I looked like a Klanswoman. None of us wore hoods, but the Druid Dionachs, or higher-ups, did have on headpieces that were a bit reminiscent of the Klan. *I don't think these outfits would fly in the United States*, I thought, *not as part of the counterculture*. But no one's face was cloaked, and there were four Black participants. Ben and Joseph, dressed in bright yellow rain slickers, raced around the crowd of sixty white-robed adults. When it was time to go, I hugged and kissed Duncan and the boys and then headed off to Stonehenge in the Druid procession. Duncan took Ben and Joseph to watch with dozens of other people from the roped-off viewing area.

The particular scenario of me on the stones while Duncan and the boys watched from the sidelines struck me as even more unlikely family-vacation behavior than what I'd done the night before. How often does a mom do something front and center that most everyone else is forbidden from doing—by British police officers, no less—while her husband and children watch? Not that often, I thought, in families featuring someone other than Madonna as the mother.

This was hardly my day in the sun, though. It was raining again, and I was shivering in my wet robe.

Metaphorically speaking, it wasn't my day in the sun, either. I wasn't a long-suffering housewife who was finally playing at Carnegie Hall to a crowd of adoring fans. Nor was I a late-blooming writer receiving a Pulitzer prize while my husband and children cheered wildly in the background. I was just a woman, from Austin, Texas, participating in a Druid ritual. I felt incredibly fortunate to be here, and I kept caressing the stone I was sitting on, as well as kissing it for King Arthur when I first arrived. But this wasn't my life's dream—certainly no one was standing by with paella. Duncan had bought a roasted chicken in town for the postritual Druid picnic, but it had leaked in the car, and chicken grease had gotten smeared all over the napkins and apples that were in the same bag. Still, he had taken the boys food shopping in town after breakfast while I took a short nap. So what if we weren't eating paella? My husband loved me, he took care of our children while I slept or did late-night rituals, and he bought delicious—if messy—picnic food.

I was on center stage while Duncan and my children were on the sidelines, but this setup made me sad on that particular day because touching Stonehenge was more Joseph's dream than my own. And despite my paella fantasy, I didn't always want to be in the foreground with husband and children quiet and supportive behind me. That dream was important because, at twenty-three, I'd never seen anything like it in real life. But I didn't have to be queen of the day every day—I just didn't want to be destined to hover endlessly in the background making snacks. Joseph played soccer the fall after we returned from Stonehenge, and I watched him happily from the sidelines. I even volunteered to be team mother, coordinating the after-game snacks brought by all the other families. *Could this really be me?* At the end of the season, the coach gave me a certificate that read: "Danna Dragons Soccer Team Mom, Fall 2000." I certainly didn't frame the certificate, but I didn't burn it, either.

Back at Stonehenge, the noon Druid ceremony went on and on for nearly three hours, and I realized that Cedric had been right: The event was indeed non–child-friendly. While the boys would have loved to touch the stones, and I would have loved to have had Duncan's take on the whole event, Ben and Joseph never could have managed waiting silently through several speeches and meditations, a Druid communion, and the passing of a laurel leaf crown from head to head. The boys, at least, were much better off racing up and down the roped-off area with easy access to the snacks that Duncan had brought along.

Finally, we began our ending procession, which took us directly by the roped-off viewing area. Rodney had coached us on the importance of a somber demeanor as we processed, and I tried to follow his instructions. But Ben and Joseph were jumping up and down in their bright yellow slickers, yelling "Mommy, Mommy, hi, Mom!" and to the crowd around them, "That's my mom—the lady with brown hair!"

I waved and blew kisses. When I got directly in front of the boys, they burst out from behind the roped-off area, grabbed my hands, and joined the procession. I smiled with joy at their bright faces, then looked over to Duncan, eager to share the happiness I felt with him.

Duncan, too, was beaming, and he began to walk along with us, but behind the ropes. Soon, though, our path broke off from his. I turned nervously to my walking partner, a fifty-year-old nurse from Brighton. "Do you think this is okay?" I asked her, gesturing toward Ben and Joseph.

"Let the children stay!" she said emphatically and grabbed Ben's other hand. "This whole event has been entirely too stuffy. Who's going to stop us? I'd like to see Rodney try to separate a mother from her children!" She held on to Ben's hand firmly so that we made a row of four: Joseph, me, Ben, and the nurse. We walked off, across the highway to the field, a mom in white among sixty other people in white, flanked by two small boys in yellow. When we got across the road, Ben and Joseph jumped on me and then we all fell down, laughing, and tumbled in the grass.

Acknowledgments

The Weymouth Center for the Arts and Humanities provided me with a quiet place to write the last sections of this book, and I'm especially grateful to Rosemary Holland, Weymouth's administrator.

I'd like to thank Robin Behn, Michael Chitwood, Cynthia Huntington, Rick Jackson, and David Rivard for early instruction in how to write. Their lessons concerned the writing of poetry, but things carried over.

I'm grateful to Kate Moses and Camille Peri at *Salon* and Jennifer Niesslein and Stephanie Wilkinson at *Brain, Child* for enthusiastically supporting and publishing my first writings on motherhood. Emily Bernard, Jenny Price, Carlo Rotella, and Peter Steinberg each gave me sharp and generous advice about the world of agents and proposal writing. Jake Morrissey was an important voice of encouragement in the last year of this project, and I thank him for many helpful—and hilarious—conversations about parenting, writing, and the mixture.

I was initially fearful that my editor, Shaye Areheart, might ask me to tone *Dispatches* down. On the contrary,

Shaye has been a strong advocate for my telling it like it is. What better support could a writer ask for? Liza Bolitzer, at Carlisle and Company, always said the right thing when I called with anxiety in my voice. And my agent, Christy Fletcher, exhibited unflagging support for this book every step of the way. She sprang into action whenever necessary, and her advice was always pitch-perfect. Katherine Beitner is a fantastic publicity director.

I'd like to acknowledge the fine teachers and baby-sitters who took care of my children several hours a day while I wrote. During the three years I worked on this book—a time involving two major geographic shifts—my sons were taught and nurtured by Amanda Adams, Carly Chapman, Gracelyn Cromwell, Courtenay Garver, Lindsay Gold, Karen Haines, Garland Hattman, Tekla Jachimiak, Janina Knoblach, Georgina Larkin, Lucy Lenoir, Tonie Lilley, John Martin, Karoline Mathewson, Layne Mottola, Kim Page, Libby Pendergrast, Mara Pfund, Jessica Salinas, Diana Stanfield, and Mandy Waid. I am deeply appreciative of the hard work each of you does on behalf of children.

As I wrote this book, I was fortunate to have a number of engaging and educative conversations about motherhood and domestic life. These exchanges of ideas, experiences, and empathy were invaluable to me—and to the writing of *Dispatches*. I'd like to thank the following people for their insights and comradery: John Adair, Becky Baker, Sabrina Barton, Kit Belgum, Robin Bradford, Wini Breines, George Bristol, Susan Cassano, Jess Chapin, Kate Connell, Natasha D'Schommer, Pam Haag, Julie Hardwick, Margie Hattori, Margaret Jemison, David Jewell, Susan Johnson, Susan Knoppow, Kathy Leichter, Lisa

Moore, Kathy Mountcastle, Sheilah Murphy, Mary Watt
New, Forrest Novy, Demaree Peck, Mara Pfund, Jay Pul-
liam, Dolly Nagy Rech, Yevette Richards, Minou Roufail,
Beryl Satter, Eve Schaenen, Louie Skipper, Fiona Somer-
set, Will Spong, Chrystal Stefani, Jeanette Stokes, Anne
Sullivan, Holly Taylor, Janene Tompkins, Greg Welch,
Betsy and Ridley Wills, and Charlotte Woody.

I am unbelievably fortunate to have several friends
who are not only empathetic, smart, and encouraging
people, but also keen and willing readers and editors.
Emily Bernard, Kai Carver, Rosanna Crocitto, Cynthia
Eller, David Franklin, Joanna Greene, Rachel Hall, Alyssa
Harad, Molly Hunt, Erik Kongshaug, Giovanna Marchant,
Miranda Massie, Lisabeth Sewell-McCain, Heidi Tins-
man, and Margaret Wrinkle all read sections or versions
of this book and gave me honest and extraordinarily helpful feedback. Alicia Erian read everything from my most
initial and tentative first sketches to this final version, and
told me—with great insight—what she thought at every
turn.

My parents-in-law, Ruth and Russell, provided childcare at critical junctures, as well as giving us fabulous theater tickets at a time when I desperately needed a break
from this book. My late grandfather, Butter, offered financial support during the last stages of the book, as well as
constant optimism. "Anything you work hard on will
bear fruit," he told me two weeks before he died. My parents, Carol and Carter, took care of my children on
numerous occasions, as well as giving gifts and loans that
made the writing of this book possible. In addition, they
have been staunch supporters of my desire to write since

my elementary years. My sister-in-law, Jordan, has been a longtime reader of my work. As a new mother herself, her perspective on this particular book was crucial to me. My brother, Baylor, is a sharp and generous reader, as well as a strong ally in everything I do. He's not afraid to tell me when he thinks I'm making a terrible mistake, and he's equally lavish with his praise. Talks with Baylor have been some of the richest of my life. And my deep appreciation to—and for—baby Miles, who has reminded me with extraordinary force how wonderful time spent with a newborn can be.

My sister, Lucy, has been critical to the writing of this book, as she is to everything else in my life. Confidante, friend, editor, skilled hypnotist, inventive nephew-entertainer, I can't imagine how I would make sense of the world without her. To my sons, Elijah and Gabriel, I offer the humblest thanks. You have given me the material for this book, but mostly you have given me joy—to a degree I never could have fathomed. I am so grateful to be your mother. To Gunther, my husband, the greatest thanks are due. Gifted parent, chef extraordinaire, astute editor—there's nothing you can't do. I know this hasn't always felt like the book you would have wanted, but you've supported me stalwartly as I wrote it, nevertheless. This book is for you, my loving and loved partner.

About the Author

FAULKNER FOX teaches creative writing at Duke University. She holds a BA in literature from Harvard, an MA in American Studies from Yale, and an MFA in poetry from Vermont College. She lives in Durham, North Carolina, with her husband and two sons. Visit her website at www.faulknerfox.com.